GCSE OCR 21st Century
Biology
The Workbook

This book is for anyone doing **GCSE OCR 21st Century Biology** at higher level.

It's full of **tricky questions**... each one designed to make you **sweat**
— because that's the only way you'll get any **better**.

There are questions to see **what facts** you know. There are questions
to see how well you can **apply those facts**. And there are questions
to see what you know about **how science works**.

It's also got some daft bits in to try and make the whole
experience at least vaguely entertaining for you.

What CGP is all about

Our sole aim here at CGP is to produce the highest
quality books — carefully written, immaculately presented
and dangerously close to being funny.

Then we work our socks off to get them
out to you — at the cheapest possible prices.

Contents

Module B1 — You and Your Genes

Genes, Chromosomes and DNA 1
Genes and Variation 2
Inheritance 4
Girl or Boy? 6
Inheritance and Environment 8
Clones 10
Genetic Disorders 11
Genetic Testing 12
Gene Therapy 13
Stem Cells 14
Science and Ethics 15

Module B2 — Keeping Healthy

Microorganisms and Disease 17
The Immune System 18
Vaccination 19
Vaccination — Pros and Cons 21
Antibiotics 23
Drug Trials 25
The Circulatory System 27
Heart Disease 28
Correlation and Cause 29

Module B3 — Life on Earth

Evolution 31
Natural Selection 32
Producing New Species 33
A Scientific Controversy 35
Human Evolution 36
The Nervous System 37
Hormones 39
Interdependence 40
Humans and the Earth 42

Module B4 — Homeostasis

The Basics of Homeostasis 43
Negative Feedback 44
Diffusion 45
Osmosis and Active Transport 46
Enzymes 47
Controlling Body Temperature 49
Controlling Water Content 51
Treating Kidney Failure 54

Module B5 — Growth and Development

DNA — Making Proteins 56
Cell Division — Mitosis 57
Cell Division — Meiosis 58
Development from a Single Cell 59
Growth in Plants 61
Stem Cells and Parkinson's 64

Module B6 — Brain and Mind

The Nervous System 66
Reflexes 68
Learning and Modifying Reflexes 70
Brain Development and Learning 71
Learning Skills and Behaviour 72
Studying the Brain 73
Memory Mapping 74

Module B7 — Further Biology

Respiration 76
Blood and Blood Typing 78
Inheritance of Blood Types 80
The Circulatory System 82
The Skeletal System 83
Health and Fitness 84
Blood Transfusions 87
Pyramids of Number and Biomass 89
Energy Transfer and Energy Flow 90
Biomass in Soil 92
Symbiosis 94
Parasitism 95
Photosynthesis 98
Rate of Photosynthesis 99
Plants and Respiration 101
Humans and the Atmosphere 103
Biotechnology 104
Genetic Modification 105
DNA Technology — Genetic Testing 108

Published by Coordination Group Publications Ltd.

Editors:
Amy Boutal, Ellen Bowness, Tim Burne, Tom Cain, Kate Houghton, Rose Parkin,
Jane Towle, Jennifer Underwood.

Contributors:
Jane Davies, Catherine Debley, James Foster, Dr Iona M.J. Hamilton, Derek Harvey,
Rebecca Harvey, Philip Rushworth, Adrian Schmit, Claire Stebbing, Paul Warren, Dee Wyatt.

ISBN: 978 1 84762 007 1

With thanks to Sue Hocking and Glenn Rogers for the proofreading.

With thanks to Laura Phillips for the copyright research.

Photographs on page 3 reproduced with kind permission from Adrian Schmit.

*Data on page 21 reproduced with kind permission from the Health Protection Agency.
http://www.hpa.org.uk/infections/topics_az/measles/data_mmr_confirmed.htm
22 May 2007*

Data on page 29 reproduced with kind permission from the British Heart Foundation © 2006.

*With thanks to the National Blood Service, www.blood.co.uk, for permission to use the
blood group data on page 87.*

*With thanks to Dr Jean Jannin - Neglected Tropical Diseases - World Health Organisation,
for permission to use the data on page 96.*

*Data on page 106 reproduced with kind permission from the Pew Initiative on Food and
Biotechnology. Factsheet: Genetically Modified Crops in the United States.*

Groovy website: www.cgpbooks.co.uk

Printed by Elanders Hindson Ltd, Newcastle upon Tyne.
Jolly bits of clipart from CorelDRAW®

Based on the classic CGP style created by Richard Parsons.

Text, design, layout and original illustrations © Coordination Group Publications Ltd. 2007
All rights reserved.

Module B1 — You and Your Genes

Genes, Chromosomes and DNA

Q1 Tick the boxes to show whether the following statements are **true** or **false**.

	True	False
a) The nucleus of a cell contains instructions for how an organism develops.	☐	☐
b) Genes are short lengths of chromosomes.	☐	☐
c) Genes are found in chromosomes.	☐	☐
d) There are 23 pairs of genes.	☐	☐
e) Genes are instructions for a cell that describe how to make proteins.	☐	☐

Q2 Some **structures** found in the human body are named below. Add them into the table in order of **size**, from **smallest** to **largest** and then match each structure to its description. One has been done for you.

Structures listed: ~~cell~~, gene, nucleus, chromosome (smallest to largest)

Table (smallest to largest):
- (smallest)
-
-
- cell (largest)

Descriptions:
- structure inside a cell where all genetic material is found
- structures that come in pairs
- the smallest unit of an individual that can function independently
- an instruction to tell a cell how to make a protein

Q3 DNA provides **instructions** that tell cells which **proteins** to make.

a) Explain what **structural** proteins are.

....

b) What role do **enzymes** play in the body?

....

c) How can different alleles lead to different characteristics?

....

....

Top Tips: Remember humans have 23 pairs of chromosomes, that's 46 in total. Chromosomes carry genes that provide instructions for cells about how to make different proteins. It's the different proteins that are responsible for all of your characteristics like hair colour and eye colour.

Genes and Variation

Q1 An organism's genes are carried in **chromosomes**.

a) How many chromosomes would you find in a human **skin** cell? ....

b) How many chromosomes would you find in a human **sex** cell? ....

c) How many **copies** of each chromosome would you find in a sex cell? ....

Q2 Explain why **children** tend to resemble both of their **parents** but don't look exactly like either one.

....

....

....

Q3 The diagram below shows the nuclei of two simple organisms that contain only **four pairs** of chromosomes. Different **alleles** are shown using different shades of the same colour.

Organism 1   Organism 2

Organisms 1 and 2 **mate**. Put a tick in the correct boxes to show the nuclei of the cells that could be produced at fertilisation.

Look carefully at the different coloured chromosomes, remember one in each pair must come from each parent.

A   B   C   D

☐   ☐   ☐   ☐

Module B1 — You and Your Genes

Genes and Variation

Q4 The diagram shows a **pair** of human **chromosomes**. These chromosomes carry a **gene** for **ear lobes**. The position of the gene is marked on one of the chromosomes in the diagram.

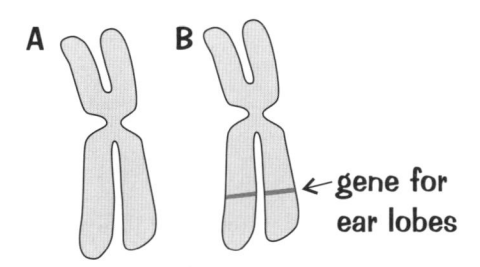

A   B

← gene for ear lobes

a) Draw the position of the gene for ear lobes on chromosome A.

b) If chromosome A came from the **mother** where must chromosome B have come from?

....

c) Chromosome A contains a **different version** of the ear lobe gene from chromosome B. Underline the correct statement below.

Sex cells contain the instructions for both versions of ear lobe.

Sex cells will only contain the instructions for one version of ear lobe.

Q5 The picture below shows two **brothers**. They have the **same parents** but don't bear a close resemblance to one another.

Complete the following statements by circling the correct word(s) to explain why two brothers (or sisters) can look quite different from each other, even though they have the same parents.

Despite inheriting **half / all / none** of their genes from the same mother and **all / none / half** from the same father, siblings don't look identical. This is because of the way **sex cells / liver cells** are made and the way they **combine / separate**. There are **tens / millions** of different combinations. Every person in the world will have **a unique / the same** combination of alleles — that's why no two people in the world are exactly the same, with the exception of **cousins / identical twins**.

Top Tips: All of this is pretty mind-boggling stuff. It's weird to think you only look the way you do because of lots of random events that took place when you were being created, apart form that dodgy haircut — you've only got yourself to blame for that.

Module B1 — You and Your Genes

Inheritance

Q1 A plant has **two alleles** for **flower colour**. The allele for **violet** flowers **(F)** is **dominant** over the allele for **white** flowers **(f)**. The possible allele combinations are shown below.

FF   Ff   ff

a) Give a definition of the word allele.

....

b) For each of the different allele combinations, say whether the plant is **homozygous** or **heterozygous**.

i) FF ....

ii) Ff ....

iii) ff ....

c) What **colour** flowers would the plants with these alleles have? Circle the correct answer.

i) FF   violet / white

ii) Ff   violet / white

iii) ff   violet / white

Q2 In cats, the allele for black fur **(B)** is **dominant** over the allele for brown fur **(b)**. Two black cats, Jasper and Belle, have a litter of kittens. Most are black, but one is brown. Tick the boxes to show whether the following statements are **true** or **false**.

                                                                             True   False

a) All the brown kittens have the alleles bb.

b) Jasper's alleles are BB.

c) Belle's alleles are Bb.

d) The brown kitten must be a mutation — all the kittens should be black.

Q3 Some people can roll their tongue and others can't. The ability tongue roll is controlled by a single gene. **Rolling (R)** is **dominant** to **non-rolling (r)**.

Izzy can roll her tongue but Saaj cannot. What conclusions can you draw about Izzy and Saaj's genetic make-up for the tongue rolling gene? Explain your answer.

....

....

....

Module B1 — You and Your Genes

Inheritance

Q4 Eye colour is controlled by the interaction of several genes. One of these genes determines whether or not a person has **brown** eyes. In this gene, the allele for **brown** eyes (B) is **dominant** over the allele for **blue** eyes (b).

Hector and Alyson are both heterozygous for this gene (Bb) and they are expecting a baby.

a) Based on the expression of this gene, write what colour eyes each offspring could have and say whether they are heterozygous or homozygous.

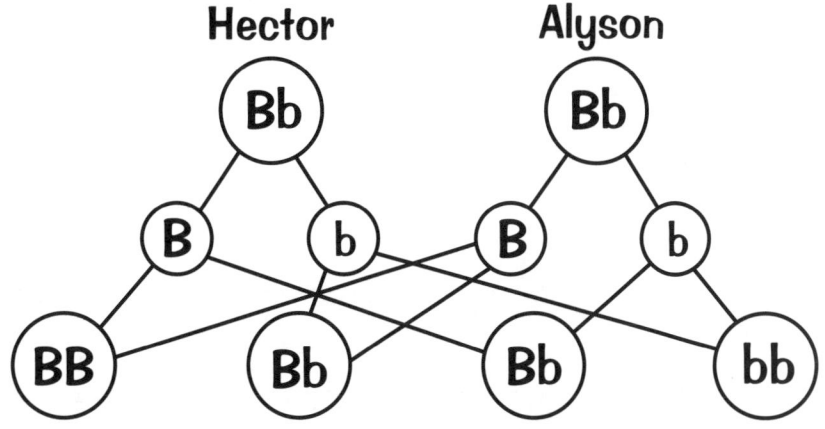

```
        Hector              Alyson
         (Bb)                (Bb)
        /    \              /    \
      (B)   (b)           (B)   (b)
       
      (BB)   (Bb)         (Bb)   (bb)
```

Colour ....

Homozygous /
Heterozygous ....

b) What is the chance that the new baby could have **blue** eyes? Give your answer as a percentage.

....

c) Hector and Alyson already have three children, they all have brown eyes. Hector thinks that this child will definitely have blue eyes. Is Hector right? Explain your answer.

....

....

Q5 In **guinea pigs**, the allele for short hair **(H)** is dominant over the allele for long hair **(h)**.

a) Is it possible for two short haired guinea pigs produce long haired offspring? Explain your answer.

....

b) Is it possible for two long haired guinea pigs produce short haired offspring? Explain your answer.

....

Would long haired guinea pigs be homozygous or heterozygous?

....

....

Module B1 — You and Your Genes

Girl or Boy?

Q1 Fill in the gaps in the passage below about how a person's **sex** is determined.

> Everybody has one pair of chromosomes that determine whether they are male or female. These chromosomes are called the .... chromosomes. There are two types, the ...... chromosome, which can be found in eggs or sperm, and the ...... chromosome, which is found in .... cells but never in .... cells.

Q2 The pictures below show the chromosomes of two people. One is **male** and the other is **female**.

Person A   Person B

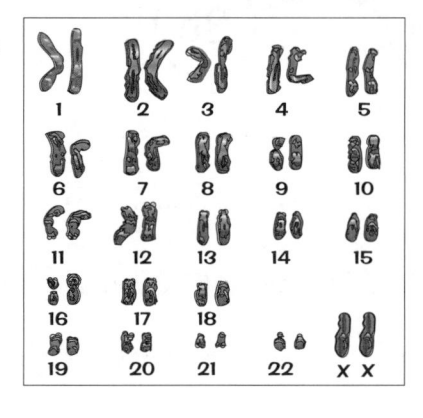

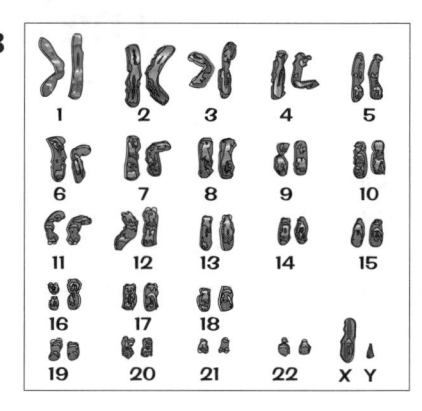

a) Which is **female**? ....
b) How can you tell? ....

Q3 The **genetic diagram** below is incomplete, fill in the spaces to show how **sex** is inherited.

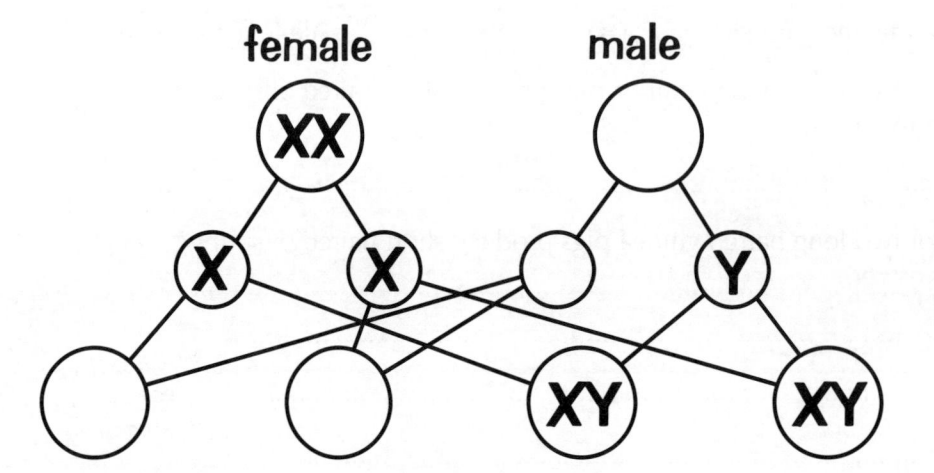

female   male
 XX   ◯
X X   ◯ Y
◯ ◯ XY XY

My son Jeremy shall inherit my stamp collection and my chromosomes.

Module B1 — You and Your Genes

Girl or Boy?

Q4 Mr and Mrs Kowalski have **three sons** and Mrs Kowalski is pregnant with a fourth child. What is the chance of this baby being another boy? Circle the correct answer.

50% 75% 10% 25%

Q5 Read the passage below and then answer the question the follows.

> The sex of a baby is determined by whether its father's sperm cell was carrying an X chromosome or a Y chromosome. On average, half the sperm cells a man produces carry an X chromosome and half carry a Y. You'd expect this to lead to equal numbers of boys and girls being born. However, in one year approximately 600 000 babies born we born in the UK. Amongst these babies, there were 20 000 more boys than girls.

From the list below, tick the boxes next to any reasons that are likely explanations for these figures.

The 50:50 ratio is only a probability and it will always vary to some extent. ☐

The data must be incorrect. ☐

Perhaps the Y sperm have a better chance of fertilising an egg than X ones. ☐

22 000 more girls would've been born the year before so overall the numbers are equal. ☐

The scientific theory that predicts a 50:50 ratio must be wrong. ☐

Q6 The sex of a developing human embryo is controlled by a **gene** that codes for the production of a **protein** called **testis determining factor** (TDF).

a) Explain how TDF controls the sex of a developing embryo.

....

....

....

b) Which chromosome do you think the gene that codes for TDF is found on?

....

Top Tips: Remember the results you get when you draw a genetic diagram are only probabilities, there's an equal chance of having a boy or a girl — though if you're anything like as unlucky as me you'll end up in a house where girls outnumber boys 3:1.

Module B1 — You and Your Genes

Inheritance and Environment

Q1 Complete the passage using the words provided.

> interaction   single   height   unpredictable   number   thousands

Characteristics controlled by a .... gene are quite rare. The majority of characteristics depend on a .... of genes working together. Because of the .... between genes there are .... of different combinations, this makes inheritance very .... is an example of a characteristic determined by a combination of genes.

Q2 Put ticks in the appropriate columns in the table below to show if these characteristics are caused by **genes**, the **environment** or **both**.

Variation	Genes	Environment	Both
Height			
Eye colour			
Hairstyle			
Skin colour			
Blood group			

Q3 **Diabetes** is a disease that affects the body's ability to control blood sugar levels. Scientists think that one type is caused by a combination of **genetic** and **environmental** factors. For each of the following statements, explain whether it indicates a genetic or environmental cause or a mixture of the two.

a) If you are an identical twin of someone with diabetes, there's an increased chance you'll also suffer from it.

....

....

....

b) Diabetes is more common in colder places, and is more likely to develop in winter.

....

c) People who were breast-fed as a baby have a reduced chance of getting diabetes.

....

d) Having a parent who has diabetes leads to a slightly higher chance of getting the disease.

....

Module B1 — You and Your Genes

Inheritance and Environment

Q4 Some diseases can be caused by both a person's **genes** and their **environment**. Read the statements about two families, the Greens and the Perkins and answer the questions that follow.

- The Greens and the Perkins live next door to each other.
- For generations, the men in both families have worked in the local paint factory.
- Mr Green has been diagnosed with cancer. His father, who also worked in the factory, died of the same cancer some years ago.
- Mr Perkins and his father are both healthy.
- Mr Green has two brothers who have moved away from the area and have different jobs. Neither man has developed cancer.

a) What evidence is there that Mr Green's cancer has been caused by **genetic** factors?

....

....

b) What evidence is there that Mr Green's cancer been caused by his **environment**?

....

....

c) What would you need to do to get a better idea whether this type of cancer is caused by genes or the environment?

....

....

Q5 The following factors are all known to increase people's **risk** of getting **heart disease**. Tick the boxes to show whether they are usually caused by **genetic** or **environmental** factors.

	Genetic	Environmental
a) Smoking	☐	☐
b) High cholesterol level	☐	☐
c) Being overweight	☐	☐
d) Having a close relative who has died of heart disease	☐	☐
e) A high salt diet	☐	☐

Top Tips: Most things are actually affected by a combination of your genes and the environment you live in, things like health, intelligence and sporting ability. Either way it means that you can blame your parents if you're a bit fat, stupid and rubbish at sport, I know I certainly do.

Module B1 — You and Your Genes

Clones

Q1 Complete the passage below choosing from the words provided.

> nucleus   growth   enucleated   dividing   physically   genetically   host   egg   donor

Clones are .... identical organisms. They can be made by scientists in the laboratory by removing the .... from an .... cell (this forms an .... cell). It is replaced with a nucleus taken from an adult .... cell. The cell is then stimulated to start .... The embryo that results from this is .... identical to the .... cell.

Q2 Jake is a keen gardener, if there's a plant that he's particularly pleased with he usually takes a **cutting** (rather than growing new plants from the **seeds**). Suggest a reason why.

....

Seeds are produced by sexual reproduction.

....

Q3 **Identical twins** are natural **clones**.

a) Explain how the way they are formed makes identical twins **genetically identical**.

....

b) If identical twins are genetically identical, what factors must be responsible for any differences between them?

....

Q4 A scientist was studying a population of plants in an area. She looked at a **mature** plant and four younger ones that surrounded it. She wanted to know if the young plants had been produced by **sexual** or **asexual** reproduction. She recorded the **characteristics** of the five plants.

Plant	Flower Colour	Leaf Colour	Seed Colour	Seed Shape
A (mature plant)	White	Green	Green	Round
B	White	Green	Green	Wrinkled
C	White	Green	Green	Round
D	Pink	Green	Brown	Wrinkled
E	White	Green and yellow	Green	Wrinkled

Which plant(s) could have been formed by **asexual** reproduction from **plant A**? Explain your answer.

....

....

Module B1 — You and Your Genes

Genetic Disorders

Q1 The family tree below shows a family with a history of **cystic fibrosis**. Both Libby and Anne are pregnant. They know the sexes of their babies but not whether they have the disorder.

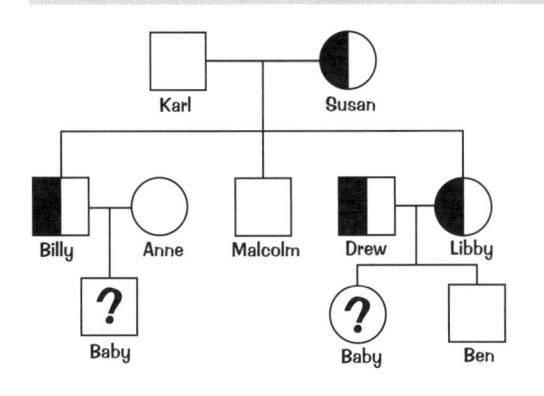

a) It is possible to have the allele for cystic fibrosis, yet not know it because you show no symptoms. How is this possible?

....

....

....

....

b) Complete the table to show the percentage chances of Libby's and Anne's babies being carriers and sufferers.

	Carrier	Sufferer
Libby		
Anne		

Sketch a genetic diagram if it helps.

Q2 **Huntington's disorder** is caused by a **dominant** allele.

a) It is possible for a person to pass the disorder on to their children unknowingly. Why is this?

....

....

b) What symptoms might someone suffering from Huntington's disorder display?

....

Q3 The table compares the **survival rates** of those born in 1960 and 1980 suffering from **disorder X**. Use this data to complete the passage below by circling the correct word(s).

Year of birth	Percentage of sufferers surviving to the age of:					
	5	10	15	20	25	30
1960	72	58	47	39	31	24
1980	89	85	79	74	69	

People with disorder X are **living longer** / **dying younger** as time goes on. Of those born in **1960** / **1980** half had died before the age of 15. About **half** / **twice** / **three times** as many people born in 1980 survived to the age of 25 than those born in 1960. The data **indicates** / **does not indicate** that people are living longer because of improvements in health care.

Module B1 — You and Your Genes

Genetic Testing

Q1 Rod and Jane are currently undergoing **IVF treatment**.

a) What do the letters IVF stand for? ....

b) Give two reasons why **genetic screening** may be carried out when a couple are undergoing IVF.

....

....

c) The embryos are screened before being implanted into the mother's womb. What name is given to this process?

....

d) Approximately 1 in every 2500 babies born in the UK will have cystic fibrosis. About 600 000 babies are born in the UK each year. How many would you expect to have cystic fibrosis?

....

Q2 Give one **objection** people have to the genetic testing of **fetuses**.

....

....

Q3 Give an example of how genetic testing could lead to **discrimination**.

....

....

Q4 **Children** and **adults** can be genetically tested to give an **indication** of their risk of getting a disease later in life. Two diseases that can be tested for are **colorectal cancer** and **ovarian cancer**. Use the information about the two diseases to say if the statements below are true or false.

- Genetic testing for colorectal cancer identifies people with a high risk of getting the disease. These people can then have regular screening for the cancer, which considerably increases their chances of survival.

- Less than half the women identified by genetic testing, as at risk of ovarian cancer actually go on to develop the disease. There is no effective screening for ovarian cancer and the only thing that can be done to remove the risk is to have the ovaries removed.

		True	False
a)	The test for ovarian cancer is not very reliable.	☐	☐
b)	Testing for a high risk of getting colorectal cancer is more useful than testing for the risk of ovarian cancer because there is no effective screening method for ovarian cancer.	☐	☐
c)	The only way to remove the risk of ovarian cancer is to remove the ovaries.	☐	☐

Module B1 — You and Your Genes

Gene Therapy

Q1 Tick the boxes to show whether the following statements about gene therapy are **true** or **false**.

    True False

a) It is readily available for a wide range of disorders.

b) It is 100% reliable.

c) It works by inserting a healthy copy of a gene.

Q2 One possible use of gene therapy is the treatment of **cystic fibrosis**.

a) Describe how gene therapy could be used to treat sufferers of cystic fibrosis.

....

....

b) Describe a **problem** associated with the treatment.

....

Q3 Some people **inherit** faulty versions of genes that make them more likely to suffer from **breast cancer**.

a) Describe how could gene therapy could be used to help these people?

....

....

b) Why can't this be done at the moment?

....

c) Why would it be possible for someone who had this treatment to still get breast cancer?

....

Q4 While gene therapy has the potential to improve lives, some people fear that it could be **dangerous**. Describe one risk associated with gene therapy.

....

....

Module B1 — You and Your Genes

Stem Cells

Q1 Tick the boxes to show whether the following statements are **true** or **false**. True   False

    a) Most cells in your body are specialised to carry out a specific role. ☐ ☐

    b) Stem cells can be found in early embryos. ☐ ☐

    c) Cells of multicellular organisms become specialised during early development of the organism. ☐ ☐

Q2 **Embryonic stem cells** have not gone through the process of **differentiation**.

    a) What is meant by the term differentiation?

    ....

    b) Suggest how embryonic stem cell research could lead to a cure for **diabetes**.

    ....

    ....

    c) **Adult stem cells** are already used in the treatment of some diseases.

        i) Describe how they are used to treat sickle cell anaemia.

        ....

        ....

        ii) Why are embryonic stem cells of **greater interest** to scientists than adult stem cells?

        ....

    d) How might a scientist culture one specific type of cell?

    ....

Q3 Many people **disagree** about the use of embryonic stem cells.

    a) Give two arguments in favour of the use of embryonic stem cells.

    ....

    ....

    b) Give two arguments against the use of embryonic stem cells.

    ....

    ....

Top Tips: Stem cells are a bit of a controversial issue. If a question pops up on the exam you must give a balanced answer, even if you have really, really strong views about their use.

Module B1 — You and Your Genes

Science and Ethics

Q1 Read the passage and answer the questions that follow.

Genetic testing of unborn babies reaches an all time high

Genetic testing can be carried out during IVF and only embryos without the faulty allele are implanted into the mother's womb. Fetuses in the mother's womb can also be tested giving parents the option to terminate the pregnancy.

Scientists have found the faulty version of the gene that causes disorder Z (a degenerative nervous system disorder) and have been quick to develop a test for it. The test has been offered since 2000. The graph on the right shows the number babies born with disease Z in country A since the test was introduced.

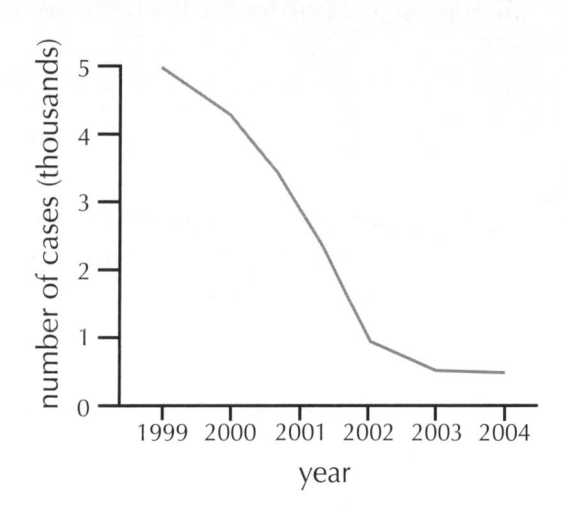

Genetic testing is not without its risks. One method of testing unborn babies is called amniocentesis — fluid from around the fetus (containing fetal cells) is extracted with a syringe and tested. If amniocentesis is carried out there is about a 1% chance of miscarriage.

Some people are against any kind of genetic testing. They think it implies that people with a genetic disorder are inferior to the 'genetically healthy'. Issues are also raised about what action to take if the result of the test is positive. Should the fetus be terminated? — Some people think that they shouldn't because they have a right to life. Other people think that they should as they might suffer their whole lives and might be a burden to their family.

Some people also think that genetic testing for diseases is a 'slippery slope' towards selecting for non-health related characteristics, e.g. eye colour. It may be possible in the future to test for the intelligence of babies before they are born. However, there are a lot of genes involved in the inheritance of intelligence and the environment has a big part to play in determining it. At the moment scientists can only test for single genes.

Module B1 — You and Your Genes

Science and Ethics

a) For country A:

   i) How many babies were born with disorder Z the **year before** the test was introduced?

   ....

   ii) Describe the **trend** shown in the graph.

   ....

   iii) Suggest a **reason** for the trend shown in the graph.

   ....

   ....

b) If **4000** fetuses were tested for disorder Z by **amniocentesis** how many **miscarriages** would you expect? Circle the correct answer.

   | 4 | 40 | 400 |

c) A couple test their unborn baby for disorder Z and it is found to carry the faulty version of the gene, which means it will have the disease.

   i) What two things can the parents choose to do?

   1. ....

   2. ....

   ii) The couple already have **two** children that **suffer** from disorder Z. How do you think this might affect their choice about what action to take?

   ....

   ....

d) The article asks, "Should the fetus be terminated". Is this a question that can be addressed using a **scientific approach**? Explain your answer.

   ....

   ....

e) i) Is it possible to test an unborn baby's genes to determine their **intelligence**?

   ....

   ii) Should intelligence be tested for? Explain your answer?

   ....

   ....

Module B1 — You and Your Genes

Module B2 — Keeping Healthy

Microorganisms and Disease

Q1 Disease in humans can be caused by microorganisms.

a) Name **four** types of microorganism.

....

b) Explain the difference between the terms **microorganism** and **pathogen**.

....

....

Q2 Circle the correct words to complete the passage below.

Many bacteria can cause an infection when they resist natural barriers, enter the body and start to **reproduce / die** — this can happen quickly because the conditions in the body are **warm / dark**. When lots of bacteria are present, they start to cause **symptoms / growth**. This can be due to bacteria producing poisons called **antibodies / toxins**, which can damage the body's **blood / cells**. Microorganisms can **never / sometimes** damage cells directly.

Q3 The human body has **natural barriers** to reduce the risk of harmful microorganisms entering the body.

a) Explain how each of the following acts as a natural barrier to microorganisms.

i) Skin ....

....

ii) Sweat ....

....

iii) Tears ....

b) **Stomach acid** can also help to prevent bacterial infections. Explain how it does this.

....

Q4 An experiment was carried out to investigate the **growth rate** of a bacterium which causes disease in humans. The experiment was carried out at 37 °C.

a) Give a reason why the experiment was carried out at 37 °C.

....

b) **Symptoms** of the disease appear when the number of bacteria reach 100 000 per cm^3. Using the graph, state how long after infection symptoms would start to appear.

....

Module B2 — Keeping Healthy

The Immune System

Q1 What is the role of the immune system?

....

Q2 Some white blood cells can produce **antibodies** to deal with invading microorganisms.

a) Can an antibody recognise a wide range of microorganisms? Explain your answer.

....

....

b) Describe another way white blood cells can help to defend against microorganisms.

....

Q3 a) Put the stages in order (1-4) to show how **white blood cells** deal with infection caused by a microorganism.

- [ ] The antibodies attach to the microorganism.
- [ ] White blood cells detect the surface antigens of the invading microorganism.
- [ ] An antibody that can attack the microorganism is produced.
- [ ] The microorganism is killed.

b) Outline what would happen if the **same** microorganism was encountered again.

....

....

Q4 Underline the correct description of an **antigen**.

A 'foreign' cell.

A chemical that causes disease. A molecule found on the surface of a microorganism. A molecule that destroys bacteria.

Q5 Two friends, Mahmood and Chris had a test to see if they needed to be immunised against tuberculosis (TB). The test measured whether they were **already immune** to TB (i.e. if they had enough antibodies specific to TB in their blood). The results showed that Mahmood had a high level of TB antibodies in his blood but Chris did not. It was recommended that Mahmood did not have the TB vaccination, but that Chris should have it.

a) Explain why Chris needed the vaccination and Mahmood did not.

....

b) Suggest a reason why Mahmood and Chris had such different levels of antibodies in their blood.

....

Module B2 — Keeping Healthy

Vaccination

Q1 Circle the correct words to complete the passage below.

Illness can be due to microorganisms **dying / causing damage** before the immune system can destroy them. If you become infected with a microorganism you have been vaccinated against, you **will / won't** have specific antibodies in your blood before the infection.

Q2 Most people who catch **mumps** only suffer mild symptoms and death from the disease is extremely rare. If most people can overcome the disease themselves, why is it considered necessary to vaccinate against it?

....

Q3 Vaccination usually involves injecting the body with a **dead** or **inactive** form of a pathogen.

Why do dead microorganisms cause the body to produce antibodies?

....

Q4 A **vaccination programme** was introduced in a country to stop the spread of **disease A**. Parents were advised to have their children vaccinated at the age of 3. Two years later, a survey was done to see the effects of the vaccination programme. The results obtained are shown below.

> Of the children vaccinated, 11% had developed the disease.
> Of the non-vaccinated children, 40% had developed the disease.
> Of the vaccinated children, 10% suffered side effects.
> In 3 cases, the side effects of the vaccination were very serious.

a) Underline any of the statements below that are **possible** explanations for the fact that the injection worked for some and not others.

The vaccine does not work.

The vaccine did not work in some cases because the children had previously suffered from the disease.

The children who did not get the disease were in better general health.

The vaccine was contaminated.

You are not expected to know the facts in questions like this — they're just to test your judgement about scientific issues.

b) Explain why vaccinations are never considered to be **completely safe**.

....

....

Top Tips: Vaccination is a really effective way of controlling the spread of a disease. There's a small amount of risk involved as the pathogen itself is injected — don't worry side effects are pretty rare.

Module B2 — Keeping Healthy

Vaccination

Q5 Vaccines for some diseases only need to be given to an individual once every 10 years. There is a vaccine available for **influenza** (flu), which is usually given to people that are especially vulnerable, e.g. the elderly. This vaccine needs to be given every year. For some diseases, like **HIV**, there are currently no effective vaccines at all.

a) Why do people have to be vaccinated against flu every year?

....

....

b) Why is it difficult to develop an effective vaccine against HIV?

....

....

Q6 A **course of vaccination** against **disease B** consists of three injections at 5-week intervals, followed by a booster injection 5 years later. The graph shows the average level of antibodies in the patients' blood over the course of the programme.

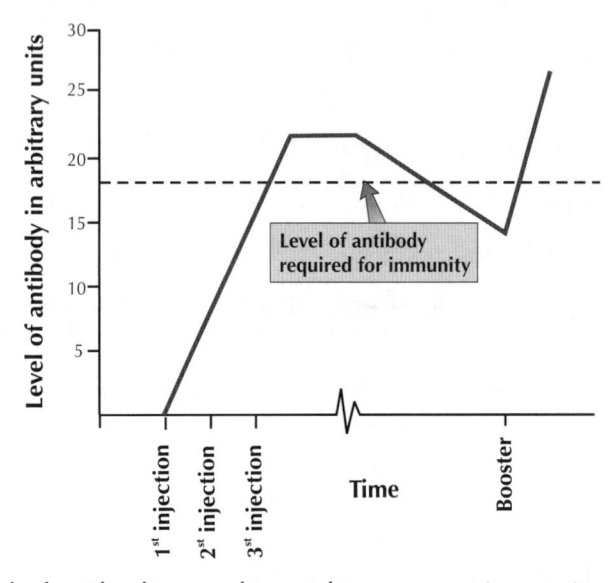

a) Explain why the level of antibodies can be used to measure immunity to a disease.

....

b) Using the graph, explain why:

i) Three injections are needed initially.

....

ii) A booster injection is needed after 5 years.

....

Module B2 — Keeping Healthy

Vaccination — Pros and Cons

Q1   Read the passage below and answer the questions that follow.

The MMR Vaccine in the Spotlight

The Government's Health Department is concerned about a possible measles epidemic as parents continue to resist having their children vaccinated against the disease with the MMR vaccine. The graph below shows the number of measles cases in the UK between 1999 and 2004.

The vaccine is given to children when they're 13 months old and protects them against three diseases — measles, mumps and rubella. Mumps can cause meningitis, sterility in men and deafness. Rubella causes little harm unless it's caught in the early stage of pregnancy, when it can cause severe problems in the developing baby. Measles is the most serious of the three diseases, as it can lead to pneumonia, fits, and even death.

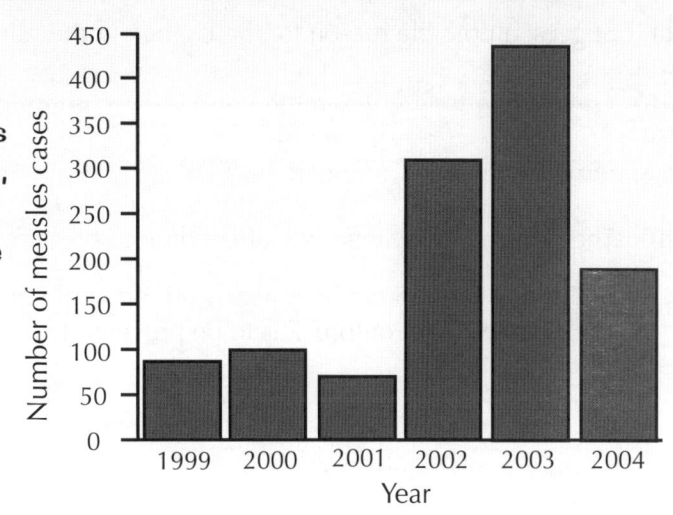

The number of children being vaccinated with the MMR vaccine each year decreased, following a paper published in 1998 which suggested a possible link between the MMR vaccine and the brain condition autism. However, many other studies across the world involving thousands of children have consistently failed to find any link between the vaccination and autism.

The Government's target is for 95% of children to be vaccinated. At present, about 85% are being vaccinated, though this is an increase from a low point of around 80% a few years ago.

Some parents would prefer to have their children vaccinated separately against each disease rather than all at once. This is not recommended by the medical authorities for the following reasons:

1. The separate vaccines have not been tested and licensed in this country.
2. It requires more visits to a surgery and there is a greater likelihood that people will forget.
3. The child has to have three times as many injections.
4. The separate vaccines have been shown to be less effective in provoking an immune response.

The MMR vaccine, like all others, can produce unpleasant side effects in some individuals. Scientists cannot categorically prove that there is no link whatsoever between MMR and autism, as some people demand, but all the evidence suggests that any medical risks of having a child vaccinated with MMR are much less than leaving the child unvaccinated.

Module B2 — Keeping Healthy

Vaccination — Pros and Cons

a) Explain why some parents resist having their children vaccinated with the MMR vaccine.

....

....

b) Circle the disease (that is vaccinated against using MMR) that is thought to be the **most serious**.

   Mumps   Measles   Rubella

c) Suggest a possible reason for the change in the number of measles cases **after 2001**.

....

....

d) The government wants 95% of children to be vaccinated.

   i) Why is it important that **nearly all** the population are immunised against a disease if an outbreak is to be prevented?

   ....

   ....

   ii) Give an argument **against** forcing 100% of the population to be vaccinated.

   ....

   ....

e) Four reasons are given against the use of separate vaccines for measles, mumps and rubella. Of these, which one do you think parents would be **most** concerned about. Give a reason for your answer.

....

....

f) The article states that, "Scientists cannot categorically prove that there is no link whatsoever between MMR and autism". Explain why this is.

....

....

g) In poorer developing countries there might not be enough money to vaccinate everyone. Circle the most appropriate way the available vaccines should be used.

   To immunise the adults in the country.

   In the way that best controls the disease.

Module B2 — Keeping Healthy

Antibiotics

Q1 Explain the difference between an **antibody** and an **antibiotic**.

....

....

Q2 Jenny went to the doctor because she had **flu**. The doctor didn't give her any drugs and advised her to stay in bed for a while. Why wouldn't the doctor give her any antibiotics for her condition?

....

Q3 In 1960, a **new antibiotic** was discovered which was very effective against **disease X**. Doctors have been prescribing this drug ever since. The graph below shows the number of deaths from disease X over a number of years.

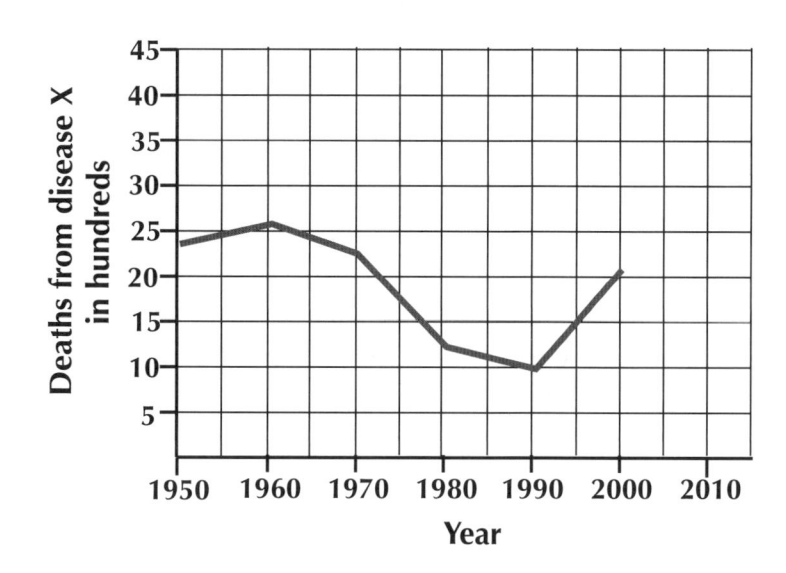

a) Assuming nothing changes, use the graph to **predict** the number of deaths from disease X in **2010**.

....

b) Suggest a reason for the **fall** in deaths from the disease between 1960 and 1990.

....

c) Suggest a reason for the **sudden rise** in deaths from the disease between 1990 and 2000.

....

Try to consider the less obvious reasons for a rise.

....

Top Tips: Antibiotics are just great but they should be used with care as nobody wants a nasty superbug hanging around, bugging everyone. You need to know how these can develop. So learn it.

Module B2 — Keeping Healthy

Antibiotics

Q4 There is concern about the appearance of **superbugs**.

a) Explain how microorganisms can develop **resistance** to an antibiotic.

....

....

b) Two things are thought to help combat superbugs:

> 1. Doctors should avoid prescribing antibiotics for minor ailments if patients can do without them.
> 2. When needed, doctors should provide a wide variety of antibiotics and not use a few all the time.

Explain how these actions **reduce** the chance of more superbugs appearing.

Action 1 ....

....

Action 2 ....

....

Q5 The graph shows the number of bacteria in Gary's blood during a two-week course of **antibiotics**.

a) How long after starting the course of antibiotics will Gary's symptoms disappear? ....

b) Why is it important for Gary to **finish** his full course of antibiotics?

....

....

Module B2 — Keeping Healthy

Drug Trials

Q1 Before a drug can be sold, it is tested on a variety of different cells and organisms. Put the cells and organisms in the order that drugs would be tested on. The first one has been done for you.

- [1] Human cells in a laboratory
- [ ] Sufferers of the disease
- [ ] Healthy human beings
- [ ] Mammals (other than humans)

Q2 Explain why, during drug trials, the following are usually tested on:

a) **Live mammals**.

....

b) **Human cells** grown in a lab.

....

Q3 Many people are **against** the use of animals for testing drugs intended for humans.

a) Give one **advantage** of testing drugs on animals.

....

b) Give one **disadvantage** of using animals, when the drug is intended for humans.

....

Q4 Before a drug is tested on sufferers, **clinical trials** are carried out with **healthy volunteers**.

a) Explain why healthy people are used to test the drug before the sufferers.

....

b) What does the term 'clinical trial' mean?

....

c) If the drug causes no problems whatsoever for the healthy volunteers, can scientists be certain that it is safe to use with sufferers? Explain your answer.

....

....

Module B2 — Keeping Healthy

Drug Trials

Q5 An on-line advertisement for a new drug states that taking it can reduce 'bad' cholesterol by 52% (compared with 7% using a **placebo**) and increase 'good' cholesterol by 14% (compared with 3% using a placebo).

  a) What is a placebo?
  ....

  b) In trialling this drug, suggest why the manufacturer used a placebo.
  ....

  c) In a study of drug effectiveness it is essential for the people who take the drug and the people who take the placebo to have certain similar characteristics. Circle the characteristics that are important, as they could affect the results.

   hair colour   marital status   age   health   income   sex

  d) Suggest why a placebo might not be used if the drug being tested was a possible cure for advanced cancer.
  ....

Q6 A new drug for a skin condition was being tested on patients that had the condition. The testers were using a **'double blind'** trial. Some of the patients were given a cream containing the drug, while others were given a placebo. Neither the patients nor the scientists were told which batch of cream had the drug in it.

  a) Why were the patients not told which cream they were given?
  ....
  ....

  b) Why were the scientists not told?
  ....
  ....

  c) If this drug is useful, suggest what results would you expect to see?
  ....
  ....

Top Tips: Testing drugs on animals is a very controversial issue. Some people think it's unethical and cruel to use animals in this way. Currently the law states that drugs must be tested on animals before they can be used on humans. A suitable alternative method is needed, before this can change.

Module B2 — Keeping Healthy

The Circulatory System

Q1 Complete the passage using the words provided below.

| carbon dioxide | vessels | nitrogen | oxygen | glucose |
| particles | veins | arteries | capillaries | tubes |

Blood is vital to the working of the body. It is carried around the body in blood ……………………. The blood is carried away from the heart in …………………… and brought back in …………………… . It supplies the tissues with …………….. and …………………… for energy, and carries …………………………… to the lungs, where it is removed.

Q2 The **heart** keeps blood pumping around the body.

a) Why is a blood supply to the heart (via the coronary arteries) essential?

……

b) What type of cell makes up the walls of the heart?

……

Q3 People are advised to lower the amount of **fat** in their diet to reduce the risk of **heart disease**.

How can a high-saturated fat diet lead to heart disease?

……

……

Q4 The pictures below show cross sections of two **blood vessels** — an artery and a vein.

a) Which blood vessel is an artery and which a vein?

A = ………………   B = ………………

b) Explain how the following structures are related to the **function** of the blood vessel.

i) Strong and elastic walls of arteries ………………………………………………………………

………

ii) Large lumen in veins ………………………………………………………………………………

………

iii) Valves in veins ……………………………………………………………………………………

………

Module B2 — Keeping Healthy

Heart Disease

Q1 Each of the factors below **increase** the **risk** of heart disease. Tick the correct boxes to show whether each of the factors are **lifestyle** factors or **non-lifestyle** factors.

		Lifestyle	Non-lifestyle
a)	Poor diet	☐	☐
b)	Excessive alcohol intake	☐	☐
c)	Family history of heart disease	☐	☐
d)	Smoking	☐	☐
e)	Stress	☐	☐

Q2 State two reasons why **regular moderate exercise** reduces your risk of heart disease.

1. ....

2. ....

Q3 Heart disease is more common in **industrialised** countries than in **non-industrialised** countries. Tick the box next to the explanation(s) below that you think are valid, reasonable explanations for this.

☐ Poorer people in non-industrialised countries die of other things before they reach the age when heart disease is most likely.

☐ People in non-industrialised countries eat less junk food and so have a lower fat diet.

☐ Poorer people in non-industrialised countries will have to walk more because they cannot afford cars and so they get more exercise.

☐ Poorer people in non-industrialised countries cannot afford the treatment for heart disease and so are more likely to die of it.

Q4 Some scientists study the **patterns of disease** around the world and how diseases spread.

What name is given to this type of study?

....

Q5 Barry has been told that he has a high risk of heart disease because he is very overweight and does little exercise. However, he refuses to start an exercise programme and says "My father was even heavier than me and never did any exercise, and he lived until he was 80".

Explain what is wrong with Barry's argument.

....

....

Module B2 — Keeping Healthy

Correlation and Cause

Q1 Read the passage below and answer the questions that follow.

In the UK today, around 13 million adults smoke cigarettes. The consequences to health of smoking are widely accepted, especially in relation to the increased risk of lung cancer. Heart disease is as great a problem but is often overlooked as a significant risk associated with smoking.

Heart disease is a major problem in Western Europe, with 268 000 heart attacks each year in the UK alone. A recent study has estimated that 29% of all heart attacks in Western Europe are due to smoking. Tobacco smoke contains around 4000 chemicals in the form of particles and gases, some of which are thought to have harmful effects on the body.

A 50 year study (study A) showed that mortality from heart disease in Britain was 60% higher in smokers than in non-smokers. The results of this study are shown in figure 1.

The study also looked at other diseases, such as cancers, in relation to smoking. Cancer is thought to be the most common form of death from smoking in the UK. The annual mortality rates from lung cancer are shown in figure 2 below for current and non-smokers.

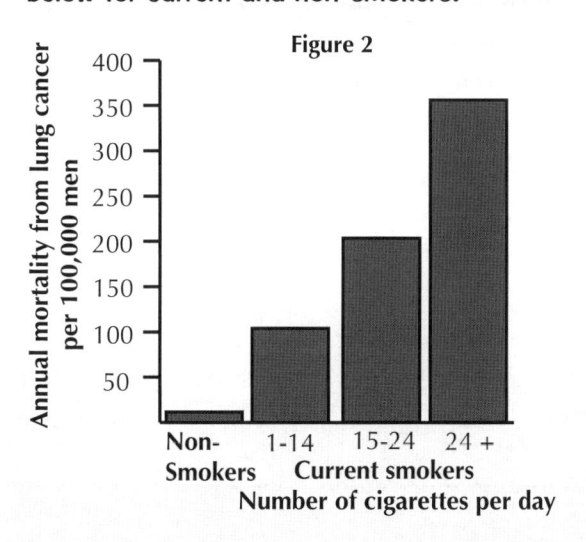

Figure 1 Study A — Annual mortality per 100 000 men

Cause of death	Non smokers	Smokers
Lung cancer	14	209
All cancers	305	656
Coronary heart disease	573	892
All cardiovascular disease	1037	1643
Chronic obstructive lung disease	10	127
All respiratory disease	107	313
Total mortality	1706	3038

Figure 2 — bar chart: Annual mortality from lung cancer per 100,000 men vs Number of cigarettes per day (Non-Smokers, 1-14, 15-24, 24+ Current smokers)

The study concluded that about half of all regular smokers will be killed by their habit. However the ill effects of smoking are not only felt by smokers themselves but also by those around them. Inhaling second-hand smoke can also be harmful to health. It is thought that regular exposure to second-hand smoke increases the risk of heart disease and lung cancer by around 25%.

A significant proportion of the UK population are regularly exposed to second-hand smoke in the home — around 7.3 million adults and 5 million children. There is mounting evidence that this can have a serious effect on health. Many potentially toxic gases are thought to be present in higher concentrations in second-hand smoke than in the 'mainstream' smoke inhaled by smokers. These gases include ammonia and hydrogen cyanide. However, only two thirds of British adults believe that passive smoking increases the risk of heart disease.

It is becoming clear that there needs to be an increase in awareness in the risks of smoking in relation to heart disease, as well as the general long term effects of passive smoking.

Module B2 — Keeping Healthy

Correlation and Cause

a) What percentage of heart attacks in Western Europe are thought to be due to smoking? Circle the correct answer.

25%   29%   50%   60%

b) Explain why should you include as many people as possible in a study of the effects of smoking.

....

....

c) i) Suggest another group of people that it would have been helpful to include in study A. Give a reason for your answer.

....

....

ii) Complete the passage below choosing from the words provided.

| minimise | exercise | body weight | maximise | height |

Studies like this must try to .... the effects of other factors.
Things like the .... of people in the study and the amount of
.... they do could also effect the risk of heart disease.

d) How many more deaths per year per 100 000 men from coronary heart disease are there in smokers compared to non smokers? ....

e) Does figure 2 show a **correlation** between smoking and lung cancer? Explain your answer.

....

....

f) A newspaper reported these findings under the headline, "Studies show smoking causes lung cancer". Explain why this headline is misleading.

....

....

g) At the moment there is a ban on smoking in public buildings in some countries, but exceptions are allowed. Many people want a complete ban.

i) Suggest one reason that would be given by campaigners for a complete ban.

....

ii) Suggest one reason that would be given for those that oppose such a ban.

....

....

Module B2 — Keeping Healthy

Module B3 — Life On Earth

Evolution

Q1 Life on **Earth** is incredibly **varied**.

a) How long ago is life on Earth thought to have begun? Circle the correct answer.

    350 thousand years   **3500 million years**   **3500 billion years**

b) How many species are there **estimated** to be on Earth today? Circle the correct answer.

    less than 1 million   **2 - 100 million**   **200 - 1000 million**

c) Circle the correct word in each pair to complete the following sentence.

The species on Earth today **grew** / **evolved** from very **simple** / **complex** living things.

d) Many more species have existed on Earth since life began than are around today. What has happened to the species that no longer exist?

....

Q2 The **theory of Evolution** is generally accepted in the scientific community because there is good **evidence** to support it.

a) How much **DNA** do humans and chimpanzees share? Circle the correct answer.

    15%   **55%**   **95%**

b) Chickens share 60% of their DNA with humans. Compare this with your answer to part a) to explain how DNA evidence supports the theory of evolution.

....

....

c) i) Give another source of evidence for evolution. ....

ii) Explain how this evidence supports the theory.

....

Q3 No one knows for sure how **life** on Earth **began**.

a) One theory is that all life evolved from **simple chemicals**. What property would these chemicals need to have in order for them to develop into living species?

....

b) Suggest two places that these chemicals could have come from.

1. ....

2. ....

c) Suggest a reason why there is no definite answer for how life on Earth began.

....

Module B3 — Life On Earth

Natural Selection

Q1 Describe the difference between **natural selection** and **evolution**.

....

....

Q2 Tick the boxes to show whether the following statements are **true** or **false**.   True   False

a) Species become better and better suited to an environment due to natural selection. ☐ ☐

b) Organisms with a better chance of survival are less likely to pass on their genes. ☐ ☐

Q3 The statements below explain the **process** of natural selection. Number the statements to put them in the correct order. The first and last stages have been done for you.

☐ This means more of the next generation have the alleles which help them survive.

☐ These organisms have a better chance of survival.

1 Living things vary slightly from each other.

☐ The species becomes better and better able to survive in its environment.

7 Over several generations, the most advantageous features are naturally selected.

☐ Some variations make an organism better suited to its environment.

☐ The organisms which are more likely to survive are more likely to breed and pass on their genes.

Q4 **Variation** within a species is needed for natural selection.

a) What two factors can cause variation?

....

b) Which of these factors can be passed on to future generations?

....

Q5 A farmer wants to produce large red tomatoes because these make the most money. He cross-breeds two varieties — one that produces large, orangey-red tomatoes, and another that produces smaller, bright red fruit.

a) What should the farmer do when he next comes to breed new tomato plants?

....

b) i) What is the process the farmer is using called? ....

ii) How is it different from natural selection? ....

....

Module B3 — Life On Earth

Producing New Species

Q1 Mutations happen all the time, but rarely produce new species.

a) What are mutations?

....

b) Suggest two factors that might cause mutations.

....

c) Mutations that are passed on to the next generation may have an effect in the offspring, or no effect at all. Explain how a mutation could cause the following results:

i) **No** effect ....

ii) A **harmful** effect ....

iii) A **positive** effect ....

Q2 Helen has skin cancer caused by a mutation that **damaged the DNA** in her skin cells. Since she developed cancer, Helen has had three children. None of her children have skin cancer.

Explain why the mutation was **not** passed from Helen to her children.

....

....

Q3 Many years ago, a population of finches lived on North Island where **small** seeds were plentiful. During a severe storm, some of the finches were blown to the neighbouring South Island where the seeds were generally **larger**.

a) The data below shows the population of finches with large and small beaks on each island 100 years after finches were first recorded on South Island. Draw lines to connect the data with the correct island.

80% large beaks, 20% small beaks

15% large beaks, 85% small beaks

North Island

South Island

b) Explain how and why the populations on the two islands have developed differently.

....

....

....

c) What environmental factor helped the two populations develop into separate species?

....

Module B3 — Life On Earth

Producing New Species

Q4 Completely new species occasionally develop when certain factors combine.

a) Which **three** of these factors can help to produce a new species? Circle the correct answers.

velocity   environmental change   mutations

predictions   extinctions   natural selection

b) Explain how each of the factors you chose can contribute to the development of a new species.

1. ....

2. ....

3. ....

Q5 There are two varieties of **peppered moth** — one with light wings with dark spots, and one with dark wings and light spots. The graph below shows the population of each type of moth found in woodland near Manchester.

a) Briefly describe how the population of the two types changed over the time shown on the graph.

     i) **Light** moth: ....

     ....

     ii) **Dark** moth: ....

     ....

b) It is thought that the changes in the population sizes resulted from pollution from the Industrial Revolution darkening the bark of trees.

     i) Which type of moth would be better hidden from predators by darker trees? ....

     ii) Explain how this might have led to the change in population sizes seen on the graph.

     ....

     ....

     ....

c) If the Industrial Revolution hadn't occurred, would the population sizes of the two moth species still have changed? Explain your answer.

....

....

> **Top Tips:** Mutations sound like they're straight out of science-fiction — when really they happen all the time without anyone noticing. Very rarely, though, new species do develop — but they tend to be only a little different from the old one. I can't see anyone making a film about that.

Module B3 — Life On Earth

A Scientific Controversy

Q1 Complete the following passage by choosing the correct words from those given.

accepted   unchangeable   foolishness   creative   imagination   changeable

> Darwin had the .... to see beyond the idea that species were .... He made careful observations of species on the Galapagos islands and applied .... thinking to come up with the idea of natural selection.

Q2 Tick the boxes to show whether the following statements about evolution are based on **data** or are part of an **explanation**.

		Data	Explanation
a)	Fossils from related animals have been found to be similar.	☐	☐
b)	Different animals may have evolved from the same ancestor.	☐	☐
c)	Natural selection is the process by which evolution takes place.	☐	☐
d)	DNA from related animals shows a lot of similarity.	☐	☐

Q3 The statements below are observations of life on Earth. **Circle** the statements that the theory of natural selection **accounts for**, and **underline** those that **conflict** with it.

- Species of finch on the Galapagos islands have different shaped beaks that suit their preferred food.
- Some species features cannot be explained by a series of smaller changes that are all advantageous.
- The fossil record shows a series of large changes — not a sequence of small changes.
- The variety of peppered moth with dark wings became more common after the industrial revolution.

Q4 Darwin's observations conflicted with the **accepted idea** about the development of species.

a) Suggest why scientists were **reluctant** to give up the accepted idea for the development of species.

....

b) Suggest why most scientists now accept natural selection as the **best explanation** for evolution.

....

c) Suggest a reason why some scientists still **disagree** with the theory of natural selection.

....

Module B3 — Life On Earth

Human Evolution

Q1 The **brain** is a very important part of the human body.

a) How does the size of the human brain in relation to body size compare with other species?
....

b) Suggest two ways that ancient humans were given a **survival advantage** by the size of their brains?

1. ....
2. ....

Q2 The diagram below shows how **modern humans** evolved from **early man**.

a) Circle all the species that exist **today**.

b) What has happened to the other species?
....

c) i) Which of the species below would you expect modern humans to be most similar to?
Circle the correct answer.

      Homo habilis   **Homo heidelbergensis**

ii) Give a reason for your answer.
....

iii) Why do all three species in part i) share some characteristics?
....

Q3 In 1912, scientists discovered bones which appeared to be from an early human. However the evidence from these bones **conflicted** with the **accepted idea** of human evolution.

a) Give two reasons why a piece of evidence might conflict with an established theory.

1. ....
2. ....

b) What effect would the discovery of **conflicting evidence** have on people's confidence in a theory?
....

c) Most of the evidence currently available supports the theory of human evolution shown in question 2. Is this **proof** that the theory is true? Give a reason for your answer.
....

Module B3 — Life On Earth

The Nervous System

Q1 Tick the boxes to indicate whether the following statements are **true** or **false**. True False

a) As multicellular organisms got bigger they became less complicated. ☐ ☐

b) Different parts of complex organisms are specialised for different jobs. ☐ ☐

c) Multicellular organisms evolved nervous and hormonal systems to coordinate and communicate between different parts of their bodies. ☐ ☐

d) The nervous system is used for slow, long-lasting responses. ☐ ☐

Q2 Complete the following passage about the nervous system by choosing the correct words.

electrical impulses   brain   stimuli   receptors   effectors   sense   heart   spinal cord

The body has .... organs which detect ....
These organs contain ...., which send signals along nerve
cells (neurones) to the .... or .... using
....

Q3 The nervous system is made up of several different parts.

a) Draw arrows between the boxes in the diagram to show the flow of information from a stimulus through the nervous system to the response.

[Diagram with boxes: Stimulus, Receptor, CNS, Effector, Response, Motor neurone, Sensory neurone]

b) Outline the function of the following parts of the nervous system:

i) Receptor cells ....

ii) Sensory neurones ....

iii) CNS ....

iv) Motor neurones ....

v) Effector cells ....

c) The sensory system is driven by stimuli. What is a stimulus?
....

Module B3 — Life On Earth

The Nervous System

Q4 Complete the table with the entries given to show the **sense organs** and the type of **receptors** they contain.

Organ	Receptor type
	Light
Nose	
	Sound / balance
Tongue	
	Touch / temperature

Ear
Taste
Skin
Smell
Eye

Q5 The nervous system allows you to react to a **stimulus**.

a) What are the two parts of the central nervous system called?

....

b) Which of the following statements best describes nervous responses? Circle the correct answer.

Fast and long-lasting   Slow and long-lasting   Fast and short-lived   Slow and short-lived

c) i) What are the two types of effector in the human body?

....

ii) How does each of these effectors respond to an instruction from the CNS?

1. ....

2. ....

Q6 Susie has been given a **box of sweets** for her birthday. She decides she would like to eat a **red** one.

Explain how her nervous system allows her to:

a) Find the red sweet. ....

....

b) Pick it up to eat. ....

....

Top Tips: There's no need to be nervous about questions on the nervous system — just remember how all the bits work together and it'll be a piece of cake. That's a victoria sponge cake with jam and cream in the middle in case you were wondering — ooh and a nice cup of tea too.

Module B3 — Life On Earth

Hormones

Q1 Complete the following passage by choosing the correct words from those given.

blood   fast   long   target   short   chemicals   air   slow   glands   impulses   nerve

> Hormones are .... which are made in .... and released into the .... They are carried around the body until they reach a .... cell where they act. Hormones are generally quite .... to act, but their effects last a .... time.

Q2 Tick the boxes to show whether the following responses are mainly controlled by the **nervous** or **hormonal** systems.

		Nervous system	Hormonal system
a)	Hearing the alarm clock and turning it off.	☐	☐
b)	Your heart beating faster when you remember you have an exam that day.	☐	☐
c)	Smelling toast burning.	☐	☐
d)	Your hairs standing on end when you're cold.	☐	☐

Q3 Rob is watching a horror film when some tense music starts. His **pupils dilate** and a few seconds later his **heart** starts **beating faster**. The tension passes and Rob's pupils return to normal immediately, but his heart takes a few minutes to slow down.

a) Describe how Rob's **hormonal system** controlled one of his responses to the scary film.
   ....

b) Describe how Rob's **nervous system** controlled his other response.
   ....

Q4 **Homeostasis** is important for keeping the body working properly.

a) What does homeostasis mean?
   ....

b) Name two body systems involved in homeostasis.
   ....

c) Describe how the body controls blood sugar levels after a meal.
   ....
   ....

Module B3 — Life On Earth

Interdependence

Q1 The resources below are **essential** for life.

a) Draw lines to connect the boxes to show which resources are essential for plants, essential for animals and essential for both.

Light   Plants   Oxygen

Carbon Dioxide   Water

         Animals

Minerals   Food

b) What would happen if an essential resource was in short supply?
....

c) Give one way that organisms are dependent on other species for their survival.
....

Q2 The following table shows the number of **rabbits** in a certain area over the last **five years**.

Year	2001	2002	2003	2004	2005
Number of rabbits	103	128	118	109	67

a) Calculate the mean number of rabbits in this area over the last 5 years.
....

b) In which year was the number of rabbits significantly lower than average?
....

c) Suggest two reasons for the decreased rabbit population in this year.

1. ....

2. ....

Q3 **Rapid environmental change** can cause a species to become **extinct**. Suggest **three** changes which could cause the extinction of a species.

1. ....

2. ....

3. ....

Module B3 — Life On Earth

Interdependence

Q4 The diagram below shows a **woodland food web**. Last year a chemical was spilt in the woods, and turned out to be poisonous to voles. The population of **voles** significantly **decreased**.

a) Suggest an explanation for each of the following consequences:

i) The population of barn owls **decreasing**.

....

ii) The population of insects **increasing**.

....

iii) The population of insects **decreasing**.

....

b) Suggest what might happen to the **bird population**. Give a reason for your answer.

....

....

Q5 The diagram shows part of a food web from Nebraska in the USA. The **flowerhead weevil** doesn't occur naturally in this area. It was introduced by **farmers** to eat the musk thistle which is a weed.

a) Why might the introduction of the flowerhead weevil decrease the number of platte thistles?

....

b) What effect will this have on the amount of wild honey produced in the area? Give a reason for your answer.

....

....

....

c) Suggest a reason why the population of platte thistles may increase as the population of musk thistles is reduced by the introduction of flowerhead weevils.

....

....

Top Tips: Interdependence is just like happy families — dad relies on mum, the kids rely on mum and dad, mum relies on Auntie Nora... Families don't tend to eat each other though, so it's not quite the same — my sister looks like she wants to eat me sometimes, but I don't think she will.

Module B3 — Life On Earth

Humans and the Earth

Q1 Tick the boxes to indicate whether the following statements are **true** or **false**.　　True　False

　a) A species is said to be extinct when there are no more individuals of that species.　☐　☐

　b) A lot of extinctions have been caused by human activity.　☐　☐

　c) Sustainable development requires that some species are made extinct.　☐　☐

　d) Humans may cause extinction directly by irresponsibly managing habitats.　☐　☐

Q2 **Human activity** can contribute to the **extinction** of animals.

　a) Give an example to show how each of the following human actions have caused species to become extinct.

　　i) Hunting ....

　　　..

　　ii) Introduction of a new species to a habitat ....

　　　..

　　iii) Destruction of a habitat ....

　　　..

　　iv) Killing of a species to protect livestock ....

　　　..

　b) Which of the actions given in part a) describe an extinction **directly** caused by humans? Circle the correct answer(s).

　　　　i)　　ii)　　iii)　　iv)

Q3 Maintaining the Earth's **biodiversity** is very important.

　a) What does 'biodiversity' mean?

　　..

　b) Suggest how the Earth's biodiversity can be maintained.

　　..

　c) Give three reasons why maintaining biodiversity is important.

　　1. ....

　　2. ....

　　3. ....

Module B3 — Life On Earth

Module B4 — Homeostasis

The Basics of Homeostasis

Q1 **Homeostasis** is an important process in the human body.

a) Define **homeostasis**.

....

....

b) Give **two** examples of conditions in the body that are controlled by homeostasis.

1. ....

2. ....

Q2 **Exercise** and **climate** can both have effects on the body.

a) Circle the correct words in the table to show the effects that **exercise** has on conditions in the body.

Temperature	increases / decreases
Water content	increases / decreases
Salt level	increases / decreases

b) What is the main risk to the body in a very **cold** climate?

....

Q3 Many **leisure activities** cause changes in the body.

Explain how each of the following can affect **blood oxygen levels**.
In your answer, name a condition that can occur during each activity.

a) Scuba-diving

....

....

b) Mountain climbing at high altitudes

....

....

....

Top Tips: Some animals don't have such a fancy homeostatic system to control temperature. Some reptiles have to bask in sunlight until their blood has warmed up before they can go about their business. I wouldn't mind lounging around in the sun for a couple of hours before work every day...

Negative Feedback

Q1 Write a definition of the term '**negative feedback**'.

....

....

Q2 The graph below shows how **negative feedback** systems operate in the body.

a) Circle the correct word in each pair to complete the sentence below.

In a negative feedback system the response produced has the opposite / same effect to the change detected — it increases / reverses the change.

b) Fill in the missing words in the labels on the graph.

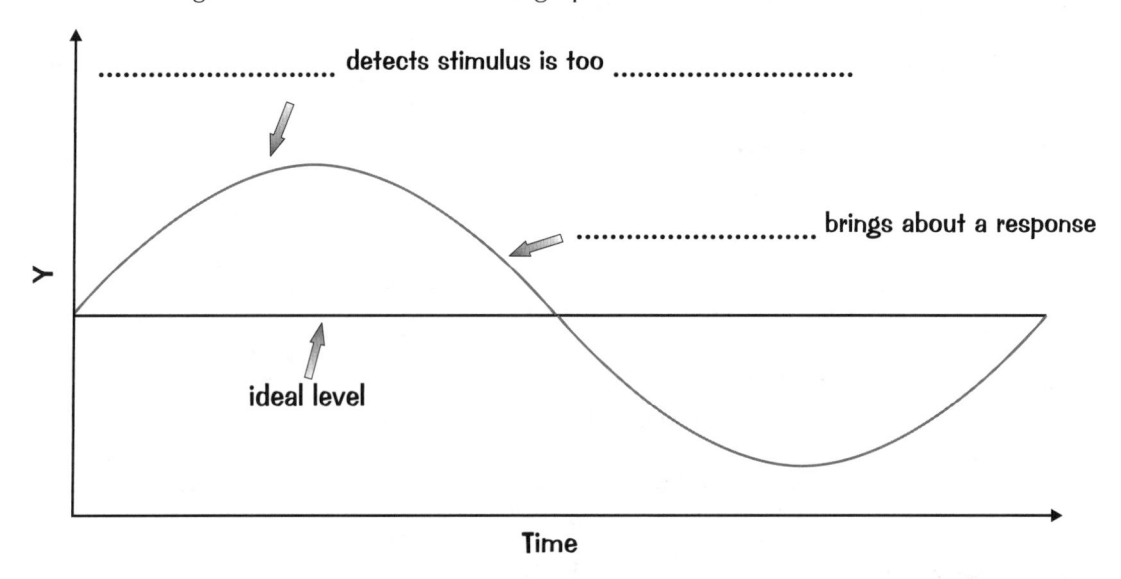

.... detects stimulus is too ....

.... brings about a response

ideal level

Y

Time

c) What name is given to the part of a negative feedback system that receives information and coordinates a response?

....

Q3 Some systems in **baby incubators** mimic natural negative feedback processes.

a) In what situation are baby incubators used?

....

b) Name a part of the incubator has the same role as the **receptor** in natural negative feedback systems.

....

Q4 What is the advantage of having **antagonistic effectors** in negative feedback systems?

....

....

Module B4 — Homeostasis

Diffusion

Q1 Complete the passage below by circling the correct word in each pair.

> Diffusion is the direct / **random** movement of particles from an area where they are at a **higher** / lower concentration to an area where they are at a higher / **lower** concentration. The rate of diffusion is faster when the difference in concentration is **bigger** / smaller.

Q2 The diagram below shows some **body cells**. A **blood vessel** lies close to the cells.

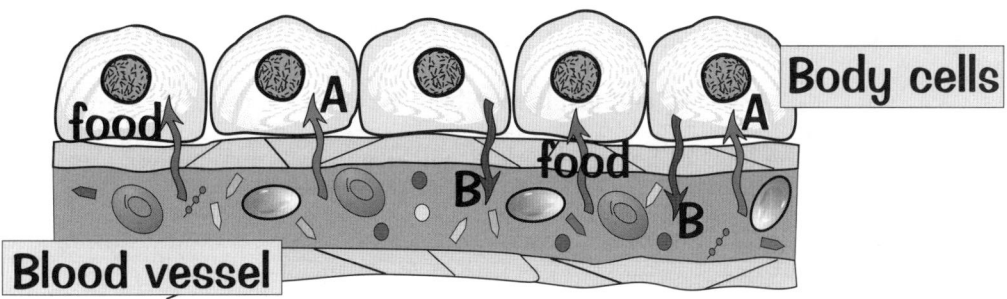

a) Is the concentration of food higher in the **blood** or inside the **cells**?
....

b) What gases are represented by each of the following:
   i) The arrows labelled A ....
   ii) The arrows labelled B ....

Q3 Tick the boxes to show whether the following statements are **true** or **false**.

		True	False
a)	Diffusion happens in gases, liquids and solids.	☐	☐
b)	Food moves from the body cells to the blood by diffusion.	☐	☐
c)	Diffusion can't happen across cell membranes.	☐	☐
d)	Oxygen diffuses from the blood into the body cells.	☐	☐

diffusion is an essential life process

Module B4 — Homeostasis

Osmosis and Active Transport

Q1 Fill in the missing words to complete the paragraph.

> Osmosis is the overall movement of .... molecules across a .... permeable .... The molecules move from a region of .... water concentration to a region of .... water concentration. Osmosis is a special type of ....

Q2 Look at the diagram and answer the questions below.

a) Predict whether the level of liquid on side **B** will **rise** or **fall**. Explain your answer.

....

....

b) What is a partially permeable membrane?

....

c) i) Describe what happens to an animal cell if it **loses** too much water.

....

   ii) Describe what happens to an animal cell if it **takes in** too much water.

....

Q3 **Active transport** is another important process within the body.

a) Define active transport.

....

b) Explain how active transport is different from diffusion.

....

....

Module B4 — Homeostasis

Enzymes

Q1 a) Write a definition of the word '**enzyme**'.

....

b) What is the name of the area of an enzyme where the substrate joins and the reaction occurs?

....

c) In the box below, draw a sketch to show how an enzyme's **shape** allows it to break substances down.

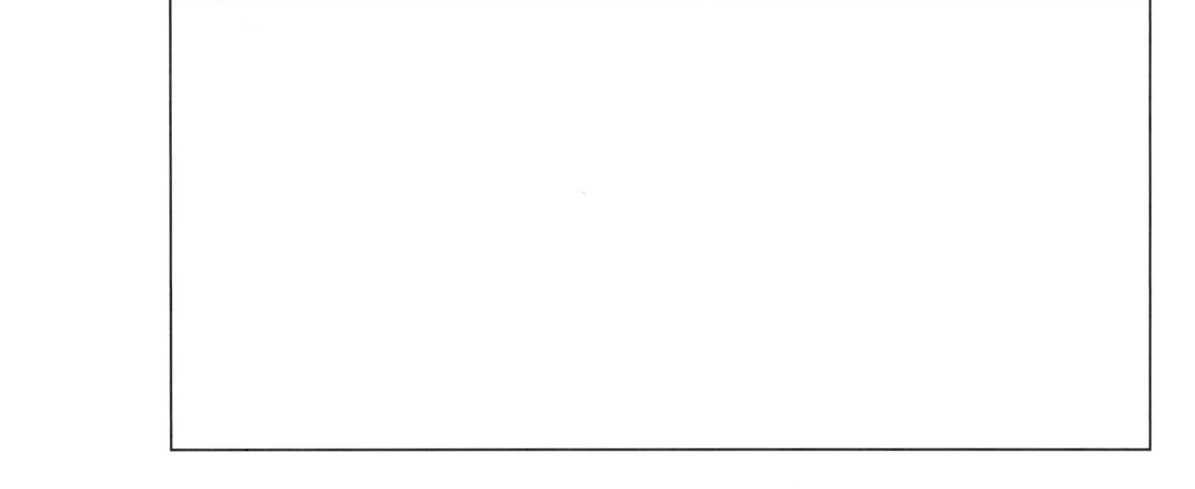

Q2 This graph shows the results from an investigation into the effect of **temperature** on the rate of an **enzyme**-catalysed reaction.

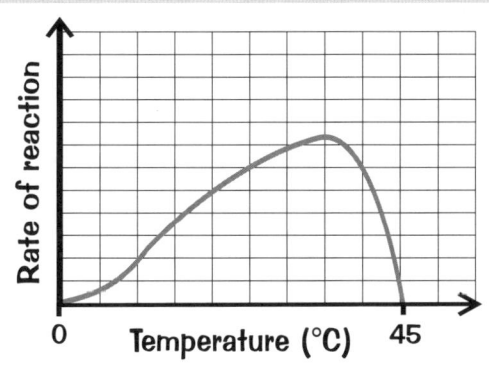

a) What is the **optimum** temperature for this enzyme?

....

b) Explain why at low temperatures a small increase in temperature increases the rate of the reaction.

....

....

c) What happens to the enzymes at **45 °C**?

....

Module B4 — Homeostasis

Enzymes

Q3 Stuart has a sample of an enzyme and he is trying to find out what its **optimum pH** is. Stuart tests the enzyme by **timing** how long it takes to break down a substance at different pH levels. The results of Stuart's experiment are shown below.

pH	time taken for reaction in seconds
2	101
4	83
6	17
8	76
10	99
12	102

a) Draw a line graph of the results on the grid below.

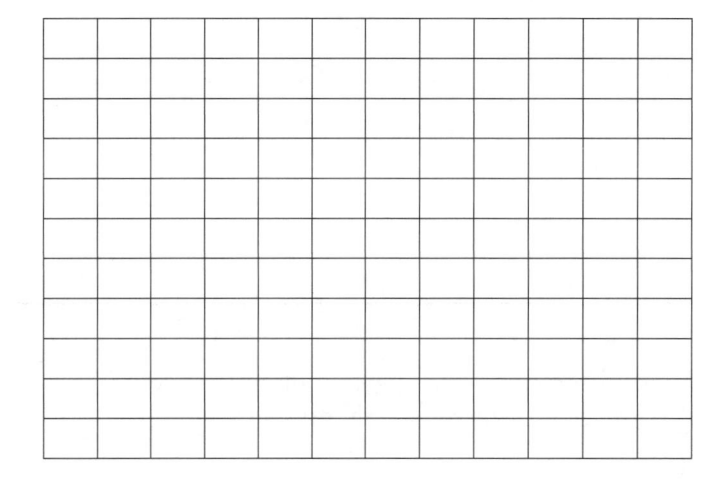

b) Roughly what is the **optimum** pH for the enzyme?

....

c) Explain why the reaction is very slow at certain pH levels.

....

d) Would you expect to find this enzyme in the **stomach**? Explain your answer.

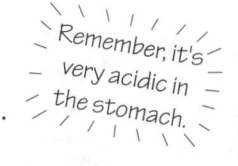

....

Remember, it's very acidic in the stomach.

e) Describe two things that Stuart would need to do to make sure his experiment is a **fair test**.

1. ....

2. ....

Top Tips: Enzymes crop up all the time in Biology so it's worth spending plenty of time making sure you know all the basics. This stuff is also dead useful if you end up sitting next to someone with Desirability for a middle name at a dinner party — nobody can resist a bit of optimum pH chat.

Module B4 — Homeostasis

Controlling Body Temperature

Q1 The human body is usually maintained at a temperature of about **37 °C**.

a) Which part of your **brain** monitors your body temperature to ensure that it is kept constant?

....

b) Name the location in the body of temperature receptors that monitor the **external** temperature.

....

c) What is the name of the **process** that enables the body to keep its temperature constant?

....

'Homeostasis' isn't the answer to this one.

Q2 The body has a number of **mechanisms** to control its temperature.

a) Which of these diagrams illustrates the skin's response to **hot** temperatures? Give a reason for your answer.

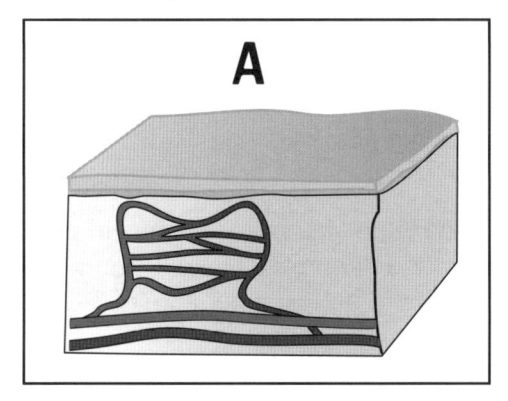

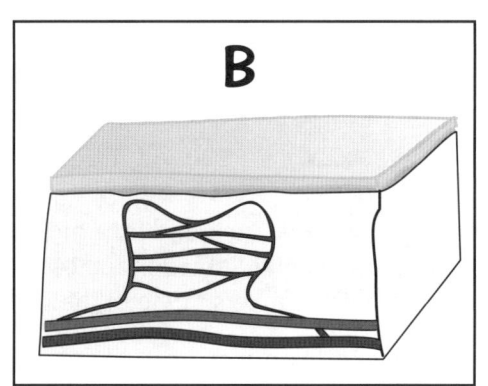

A

B

Diagram .... because ....

....

b) What other process can help the body to **cool down** when it's too hot?

....

c) Shivering can help the body to **warm up** when it's too cold.

   i) Which parts of the body are the **effectors** in shivering?

   ....

   ii) Explain how shivering helps to increase body temperature.

   ....

   ....

Module B4 — Homeostasis

Controlling Body Temperature

Q3 A holiday maker with severe **heat stroke** is admitted to a hospital in Mexico.

a) List three possible **causes** of the patient's heat stroke.

1. ....
2. ....
3. ....

In Mexico, really hot Chilli can be a cause of heat stroke.

b) Circle the **symptoms** below that you might expect the patient to exhibit.

dizziness   headache   diarrhoea   confusion   muscle pain   increased urine output

c) What happens to the normal mechanisms for controlling body temperature when you get too hot?

....

d) Describe how you would expect the patient to be **treated** when they first arrive at the hospital.

....
....
....

Q4 A group of **walkers** are found by a mountain rescue team after being missing in **poor weather** conditions on Mount Snowdon for **14 hours**. The mountain rescue team begin to assess the condition of the walkers. One of the walkers has a core body temperature of 34 °C.

a) Name the condition that the walker is suffering from.

....

b) Describe the **symptoms** the walker might exhibit.

....
....

c) Tick the correct boxes to show which of these **treatments** the patient should be given.

☐ Warm, dry clothing
☐ Placed into a bath of very hot water
☐ Warmed by a gentle heat source
☐ Exposed to very high temperatures, e.g. sitting in front of a roaring fire
☐ Have their hands and feet vigorously rubbed to warm up the extremities

Module B4 — Homeostasis

Controlling Water Content

Q1 My brother was getting on my nerves, so I put him on a treadmill and turned the setting to high (just to keep him quiet for a bit).

Will my brother lose **more** or **less** water from the following body parts than he would if he sat still? Explain your answers.

a) Skin ....

....

b) Lungs ....

....

c) Kidneys ....

....

Q2 Mrs Finnegan had the **concentration of ions** in her **urine** measured on two days.

Date	6th December	20th July
Average air temperature (°C)	8	24
Ion concentration in urine (mg/cm^3)	1.5	2.1

Assuming Mrs Finnegan consumes the same amount of food and drinks and does the same amount of exercise every day, suggest a reason for the different ion concentrations in her urine.

....

....

Q3 The body needs to balance its water input and output.

a) Why is it important to maintain a balanced water level?

....

b) Name three ways that water is **gained** by the body.

1. .... 2. .... 3. ....

c) Name two **drugs** that can interfere with your body's water level.

1. .... 2. ....

Module B4 — Homeostasis

Controlling Water Content

Q4 The **concentration** of urine and **amount** of urine produced are affected by many factors.

a) List three things that affect the **amount** and **concentration** of urine.

1. ....

2. ....

3. ....

b) Complete the following sentences by circling the correct word(s).

i) When you drink too little you will produce **concentrated** / **dilute** urine.

ii) On a hot day you will produce **more concentrated** / **less concentrated** urine than on a cold day.

iii) Drinking a lot of water will produce a **large** / **small** amount of urine.

iv) Drinking a lot of water will produce **dilute** / **concentrated** urine.

v) Exercising will produce **more concentrated** / **less concentrated** urine than resting will.

c) Why does **exercising** change the concentration of urine produced?

....

....

Q5 Some of the substances contained in the blood that enters the kidneys are listed below:

salt   water   sugar   urea   blood cells

a) List the things that are:

i) filtered out of the blood ....

ii) reabsorbed ....

iii) released in the urine ....

b) Is glucose reabsorbed back into the blood by diffusion or active transport?

....

c) Explain why the process you named in part **b)** is used.

....

....

Top Tips: Kidneys do loads of important jobs and that's why kidney failure is so dangerous. You can live with only one kidney though — so it's possible for some people with kidney failure to receive a donated kidney from a member of their family or from another suitable donor (see page 54).

Module B4 — Homeostasis

Controlling Water Content

Q6 The concentration of water in the blood is adjusted by the **kidneys**. They ensure that the water content never gets **too high** or **too low**.

a) What is the name given to the kind of mechanism by which water content is regulated?

....

b) The hormone **ADH** is needed to control the body's water content. What do the letters ADH stand for?

....

The new kidney opera house was less popular than the old one.

c) Complete the diagram below by circling the correct word in each pair.

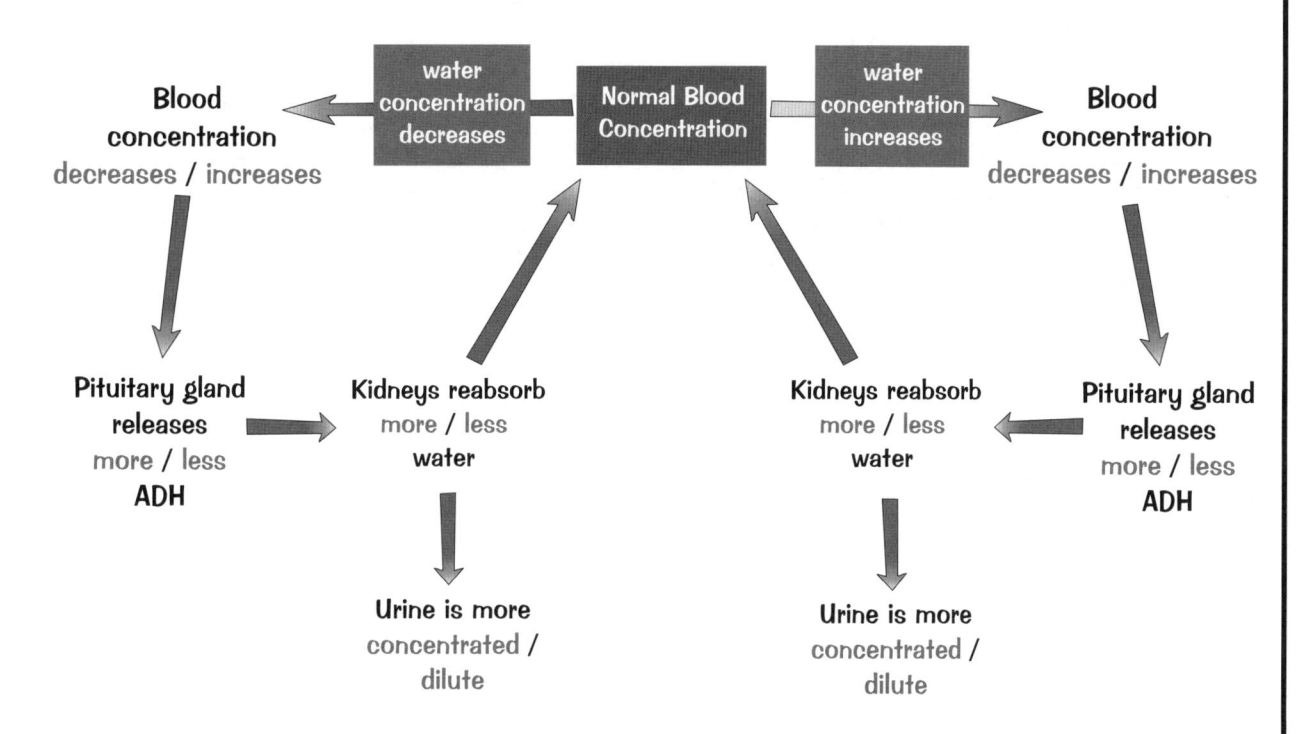

Blood concentration decreases / increases ← water concentration decreases ← **Normal Blood Concentration** → water concentration increases → **Blood concentration** decreases / increases

↓ ↓
Pituitary gland releases more / less **ADH** → **Kidneys reabsorb** more / less **water** **Kidneys reabsorb** more / less **water** ← **Pituitary gland releases** more / less **ADH**

↓ ↓
Urine is more concentrated / dilute **Urine is more** concentrated / dilute

Q7 **Drugs** can affect the water content of the body.

a) Circle the correct word from each pair to complete the passage about the effect of **alcohol** on the water content of the body.

Alcohol **increases** / **decreases** the amount of ADH produced, causing the kidneys to reabsorb **more** / **less** water than they usually do. This **increases** / **decreases** the amount of water that leaves the body as **urine** / **sweat**, which can lead to **dehydration** / **overhydration**.

b) Explain how the drug **ecstasy** can affect the quantity and concentration of urine produced.

....

....

Module B4 — Homeostasis

Treating Kidney Failure

Q1 Read the passage below and then answer the questions that follow.

Treating Kidney Failure

Around 40 000 people in the UK suffer from serious kidney failure. When the kidneys aren't working properly, waste substances build up in the blood. Without treatment kidney failure is eventually fatal.

Two key treatments are currently available for patients with kidney failure: dialysis — where machines do some of the jobs of the kidneys, or a kidney transplant.

Dialysis

Dialysis has to be performed regularly to keep the concentrations of dissolved substances in the blood at normal levels, and to remove waste substances.

In a dialysis machine (see diagram below) the person's blood flows alongside a partially permeable membrane, surrounded by a special dialysis fluid. The membrane is permeable to things like ions and waste substances, but not to big molecules like proteins — this mimics the membranes in a healthy kidney. The dialysis fluid has the same concentration of dissolved ions and glucose as healthy blood. This means that useful dissolved ions and glucose won't be lost from the blood during dialysis. Only waste substances (such as urea) and excess ions and water diffuse across the barrier.

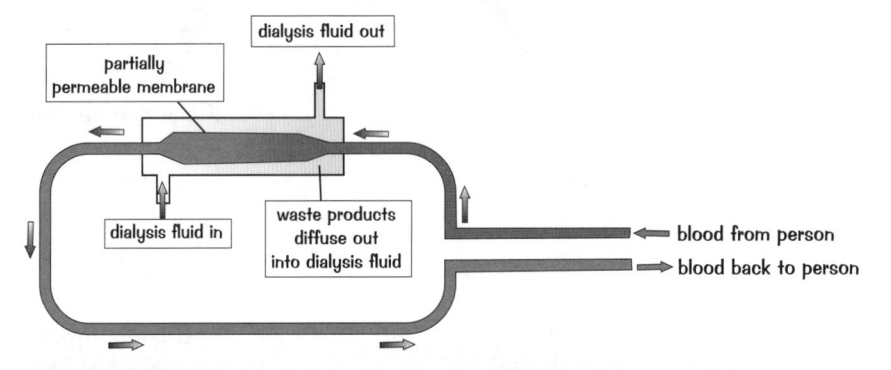

Patients with kidney failure generally need to have a dialysis session three times a week. Dialysis can be a very time-consuming process — each session can take over 3 hours.

Transplantation

Some patients are offered a kidney transplant. Healthy kidneys are usually transplanted from people who have died suddenly, and who are on the organ donor register or carry a donor card (provided their relatives give the go-ahead). Kidneys can also be transplanted from live donors — as we all have two of them and can live with just one.

Kidney transplantation has a high success rate but sometimes the donor kidney is rejected by the patient's immune system. The risk of rejection is minimised in the following ways:

- A donor with a tissue type that closely matches the patient is chosen.
- The patient's bone marrow is zapped with radiation to stop white blood cells being produced — so they won't attack the transplanted kidney. They also have to take drugs that suppress the immune system.

Module B4 — Homeostasis

Treating Kidney Failure

a) A model of **dialysis** is shown below. No movement of substances has taken place yet.

   i) Which two particles will **not** diffuse across the membrane from the bloodstream into the dialysis fluid?

   ....

   ii) Explain your answer.

   ....
   ....

   iii) Which substance's concentration will **increase** in the dialysis fluid?

   ....

   iv) What do you notice about the concentration of **glucose** on either side of the membrane? Suggest a reason for this.

   ....
   ....

b) The steps in dialysis are listed below. Number the steps in the correct order by writing 1 to 5 in the boxes.

   ☐ Excess water, ions and wastes are filtered out of the blood and pass into the dialysis fluid.

   ☐ The patient's blood flows into the dialysis machine and between partially permeable membranes.

   ☐ Blood is returned to the patient's body via a vein in their arm.

   ☐ Dialysis continues until nearly all the waste and excess substances are removed.

   ☐ A needle is inserted into a blood vessel in the patient's arm to remove blood.

c) i) Explain the advantage that a transplant has over dialysis for a patient with kidney failure.

   ....

   ii) Give **two** precautions used to try and prevent a patient's body from rejecting a new kidney.

   1. ....
   2. ....

Module B4 — Homeostasis

DNA — Making Proteins

Q1 The following questions are about **DNA**.

a) What is the **function** of DNA?

....

b) What name is given to the **shape** of a DNA molecule? ....

c) How many different bases make up the DNA structure? ....

d) Which bases pair up together?

....

Q2 Tick the boxes to show whether the following statements are **true** or **false**.

		True	False
a)	Genes are sections of DNA that code for specific proteins.	☐	☐
b)	Each amino acid is coded for by a set of four base pairs.	☐	☐
c)	Each cell contains different genes, which is why we have different types of cell.	☐	☐
d)	Proteins are made at ribosomes.	☐	☐
e)	RNA is a messenger molecule that communicates between DNA and the ribosomes.	☐	☐
f)	RNA contains two strands, like DNA.	☐	☐

Q3 On the section of **DNA** shown:

```
A G G C T A G C C A A T C G C C G A A G C T C A
| | | | | | | | | | | | | | | | | | | | | | | |
T C C G A T C G G T T A G C G
```

a) Complete the lower sequence of bases.

b) Calculate how many **amino acids** this section of DNA codes for.

....

Q4 Answer the following questions to explain how a section of code on a **DNA molecule** can be used to build a new **protein**.

a) How is a molecule of **messenger RNA** formed from a molecule of DNA?

....

....

b) How do **RNA** and **ribosomes** work together to build proteins?

....

....

Cell Division — Mitosis

Q1 Decide whether the following statements are **true** or **false**.

    True False

a) As a cell grows the number of organelles increases.

b) Chromosomes are found in the cytoplasm of a cell.

c) Before a cell divides by mitosis, it duplicates its DNA.

d) Mitosis is where a cell divides to create two genetically identical copies.

e) Nucleotides are made up of chains of DNA.

f) Organisms use mitosis in order to grow.

g) Organisms do not use mitosis to replace damaged cells.

Q2 Complete the following passage using the words below.

    nucleotides   chromosomes   DNA strands   bases   cross-links

Before a cell splits in two by mitosis, everything in the cell is copied. To copy ...., the molecule of DNA splits, then the bases on free-floating .... pair up with matching bases on the single strands of DNA. Once matched, ... form between the .... and the old ...., and the nucleotides on the new strand are joined together.

Q3 The following diagram shows the different stages of **mitosis**. Write a short description to explain each stage.

a) ....

b) ....

c) ....

d) ....

e) ....

Module B5 — Growth and Development

Cell Division — Meiosis

Q1 Tick the boxes below to show which statements are true of **mitosis**, **meiosis** or **both**.

		Mitosis	Meiosis
a)	Halves the number of chromosomes.	☐	☐
b)	Chromosomes line up in the centre of the cell.	☐	☐
c)	Forms cells that are genetically different.	☐	☐
d)	In humans, it only happens in the reproductive organs.	☐	☐

Q2 Draw lines to match the descriptions of the stage of **meiosis** to the right diagram below. The first one has been done for you.

a) — The pairs are pulled apart, mixing up the mother's and father's chromosomes into the new cells. This creates genetic variation.

b) Before the cell starts to divide it duplicates its DNA to produce an exact copy.

c) There are now four gametes, each containing half the original number of chromosomes.

d) For the first meiotic division the chromosomes line up in their pairs across the centre of the cell.

e) The chromosomes line up across the centre of the nucleus ready for the second division, and the left and right arms are pulled apart.

Q3 During sexual reproduction, two **gametes** combine to form a new individual.

a) What are gametes? ....

b) Explain why gametes have **half** the usual number of chromosomes.

....

....

Top Tips: I've tried for ages to come up with a good way of remembering which is mitosis and which is meiosis. Unfortunately I got stuck at "My toes(ies) grow(sies)...", which is rather lame if I may say so myself. I hope for your sake you come up with something better. Good luck...

Module B5 — Growth and Development

Development from a Single Cell

Q1 The following terms are related to **stem cells**. Explain what each term means.

a) specialised cells ....

b) differentiation ....

c) undifferentiated cells ....

Q2 How are **embryonic** stem cells different from **adult** stem cells?

....

....

....

Q3 Describe a way that **stem cells** are currently used in **medicine**.

....

....

....

Raymond pondered how long his bone marrow would take to grow.

Q4 Some **stem cells** are extracted from a **cloned** embryo. Number the stages in the correct order to show how a cloned embryo is produced. The first one has been done for you.

- **1** Take an egg cell.
- ...... Grow the embryo.
- ...... Insert a complete set of chromosomes from the adult you want to clone.
- ...... Remove the genetic material.
- ...... Stimulate the cell under the right conditions to reactivate certain genes.
- ...... Extract embryonic stem cells.

Top Tips: Stem cells are cutting-edge stuff right now. You'll probably see loads more of them in the news in the future as scientists use them to try to find new cures for disorders like Parkinson's.

Module B5 — Growth and Development

Development from a Single Cell

Q5 Circle the cell types below that are **specialised**.

differentiated cell   gamete   red blood cell

embryonic stem cell   nerve cell

Q6 Tick the correct boxes to show whether the following statements are **true** or **false**.

		True	False
a)	Cells in an early embryo are unspecialised.	☐	☐
b)	Blood cells are undifferentiated.	☐	☐
c)	Nerve cells are specialised cells.	☐	☐
d)	Adult stem cells are as versatile as embryonic stem cells.	☐	☐
e)	Stem cells in bone marrow can differentiate into any type of cell.	☐	☐

Q7 In the future, **embryonic stem cells** might be used to replace faulty cells in sick people. Match the problems below to the potential cures which could be made with stem cells.

diabetes   heart muscle cells

paralysis   insulin-producing cells

heart disease   brain cells

Alzheimer's   nerve cells

Q8 Explain how scientists try to get cultures of one **specific** type of cell from **embryonic stem cells**.

....

....

....

Q9 What is the **advantage** of treating a disease using stem cells from **cloned** embryos that are genetically identical to the patient?

....

....

Module B5 — Growth and Development

Growth in Plants

Q1 Give two differences in **growth** between plants and animals.

1. ....
2. ....

Q2 Decide whether the following statements are **true** or **false**.

		True	False
a)	Meristem tissue at the tips of stems contains the plant equivalent of adult stem cells.	☐	☐
b)	The cells in the meristem lose their properties as the plant ages.	☐	☐
c)	Meristem tissue is generated in the stem of the plant and transported to the roots and shoots where it is needed for growth.	☐	☐
d)	Cells produced by dividing meristem cells can differentiate to become cells in flowers.	☐	☐
e)	Differentiation is triggered by turning certain genes on or off.	☐	☐
f)	Cells behind the meristem tissue grow via cell elongation.	☐	☐

Q3 Three **plant shoots** were set up with a **light stimulus**. The diagram shows the shape of each shoot before and after.

a) Which part of the plant shoot is most sensitive to light?

....

b) Which plant **hormone** controls the growth of the tip?

....

c) On each picture, shade in the region that contains the **most** of this hormone.

Q4 **Phototropism** is necessary for the survival of plants.

a) Explain what **positive** and **negative** phototropism are.

....

....

b) Explain why phototropism is needed for a plant to survive.

....

....

Module B5 — Growth and Development

Growth in Plants

Q5 Decide whether the following statements are **true** or **false**.

a) Plant shoots grow away from light.

b) Plant roots grow towards light.

c) Positive phototropism ensures that roots grow deep into the soil for nutrients.

d) If the tip of a shoot is removed, the shoot may stop growing.

Q6 Sally takes **two cuttings** from her favourite plant and tries to **grow both** using rooting powder to produce new plants. One cutting grows **well** but the other **doesn't**. Which of the cuttings shown would you expect to **grow best**, and why?

....

....

....

cutting 1

cutting 2

Q7 Arnold placed some **seedlings** in a closed shoe box which had a small hole in the top to let light in. He left them in the box for **five days**. The change in the appearance of one of the seedlings is shown in the diagram below.

a) Label the root and the shoot on each of the diagrams.

b) Where are the hormones that cause the root and shoot to grow differently produced?

....

c) Explain the results observed for the shoot and the root in terms of their response to **light**.

i) the shoot ....

....

ii) the root ....

....

Top Tips: You often hear about athletes being caught by random drugs tests for using hormones to beef themselves up a bit — I've never heard of any gardeners having their prize vegetable carted off for a random auxin testing though. Hmmmm...

Module B5 — Growth and Development

Growth in Plants

Q8 Barry is investigating the effect of **auxin concentration** on the growth of the roots in some **identical plant cuttings**. His measurements are shown in the table.

a) What are plant cuttings? ....

The table shows the effect of auxin concentration on root growth over a week.

Concentration of auxin (parts per million)	0	0.001	0.01	0.1	1
Increase of root length (mm)	6	12	8	3	1

b) Plot a bar chart of the increase in root length against the concentration of auxin on the grid below.

c) What do the results suggest is the best concentration of auxin to use to encourage growth?

....

d) What do you notice about the effect of high auxin concentration on the rate of growth?

....

....

e) Give one thing that Barry should have done to make the test fair.

....

Q9 Two shoot tips were removed from young plants. Agar blocks **soaked in auxin** were placed on the **cut ends** of the **shoots** as shown in the diagram, and they were placed in the dark. The auxin **soaks** into the stem where the block touches it.

a) Describe the expected responses of shoots A and B to this treatment.

i) Shoot A ....

ii) Shoot B ....

b) Explain your answers.

i) Shoot A ....

....

ii) Shoot B ....

....

Module B5 — Growth and Development

Stem Cells and Parkinson's

Q1 Read the passage about using **stem cells** to treat **Parkinson's**, then answer the questions that follow.

Stem cells have been one of the decade's hottest research topics, but have so far not lived up to their promise of being a wonder-cure. However, there have recently been promising results from studies using both adult and embryonic stem cells to treat Parkinson's disease.

Symptoms of Parkinson's disease include shaking movements, muscle stiffness and difficulty in moving. Parkinson's can also cause problems with handwriting, speech and balance, leaving many sufferers with a poor quality of life.

The symptoms of Parkinson's are caused by the death of nerve cells that produce a chemical called dopamine. Dopamine carries signals in the parts of the brain controlling movement — as the levels decline, sufferers' ability to control their movements decreases.

There is currently no cure for Parkinson's disease. Symptoms can be controlled in the short term with drugs, deep-brain stimulation, physiotherapy or the implantation of healthy dopamine-producing cells from aborted fetuses.

A recent study of a new treatment showed that adult stem cells could be made to differentiate to replace the dead dopamine-producing nerve cells. The stem cells were removed from a healthy area of each patient's brain and implanted into the area damaged by Parkinson's. Once transplanted, the nerve cells began to differentiate into dopamine-producing cells as hoped. However, the cells then started to die. Unless this death of the new cells can be prevented this treatment is not a permanent cure.

Treatments using embryonic stem cells haven't been tried on humans yet, but there have been good results from studies with rats. In one study, two groups of rats were given a drug that killed the dopamine-producing nerve cells in their brains, giving them a condition like Parkinson's. One group of rats was treated by implanting embryonic stem cells in the damaged area of their brains — the other group weren't treated and were used as a control. The rats' symptoms were studied for nine weeks after treatment. The results are shown on the graph.

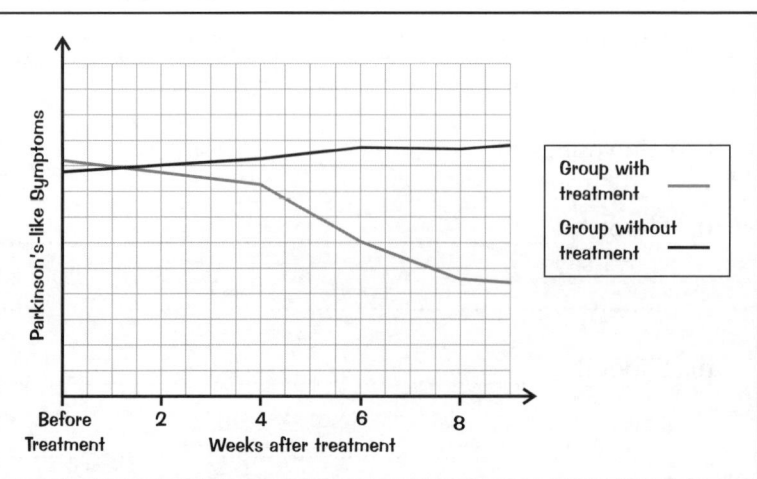

These studies show that more research is needed to realise the potential of stem cells, and that they may well provide a cure for Parkinson's and other diseases in the future.

Module B5 — Growth and Development

Stem Cells and Parkinson's

a) Give **three** common symptoms of Parkinson's disease.

....

b) A current treatment for Parkinson's is to transplant brain tissue from fetuses aborted 8 to 12 weeks after conception. Why would these fetuses **not** be suitable for the collection of stem cells?

....

....

c) In the study using embryonic stem cells, the rats were given anti-rejection drugs to stop them rejecting the implanted cells. Why wasn't this needed in the **human** study using **adult** stem cells?

....

....

d) What was the key **problem** found in the human study using adult stem cells to treat Parkinson's? Circle the correct answer.

- The patients' immune systems rejected the implanted stem cells.
- The stem cells died soon after they were transplanted into the patients' brains.
- The stem cells didn't differentiate into the right kind of nerve cell.
- The scientists had great difficulty collecting healthy stem cells.

e) The graph in the article shows the level of Parkinson's-like symptoms in the two groups of rats.

  i) Compare the level of symptoms in the two groups of rats **before** the treatment.

  ....

  ii) Describe the **trend** in the data from the group of rats given the **stem cell treatment**.

  ....

  ....

  iii) Which of the following **conclusions** would you draw from the graph? Circle the correct answer.

  - The treatment eventually cured the treated group of rats of their Parkinson's-like symptoms.
  - The treatment made the treated group of rats' Parkinson's-like symptoms progressively worse over time.
  - The treatment was effective in reducing the level of Parkinson's-like symptoms in the group of rats treated.
  - The treatment would gradually reduce the level of Parkinson's symptoms in humans if used on humans.

Module B5 — Growth and Development

Module B6 — Brain and Mind

The Nervous System

Q1 Complete the following passage using words from the box.

> environment   favourable   change   mate
> stimulus   respond   temperature   danger

A .... is any .... in the ....
of an organism, for example a change in air .... It's important
that organisms .... to stimuli to keep themselves in
.... conditions, for example to avoid ....
or when finding a ....

Q2 The **CNS** makes up part of the **nervous system**.

a) What do the letters **CNS** stand for? ....

b) What is the **function** of the CNS?
....

c) On the diagram label the parts that make up the CNS.

d) What is the role of the **peripheral** nervous system?
....
....

e) What type of neurones:

i) carry information **to** the CNS? ....

ii) carry instructions **from** the CNS? ....

Q3 Put the words below into the correct columns in the table to show the different types of effectors and receptors, and the different **organs** they form part of.

sound receptor cells   ~~taste buds~~   muscle cells   glands   the ear   light receptor cells   muscles   ~~the tongue~~   the eye   hormone secreting cells

	Example	Make up part of...
Receptor	taste buds	the tongue
Effector		

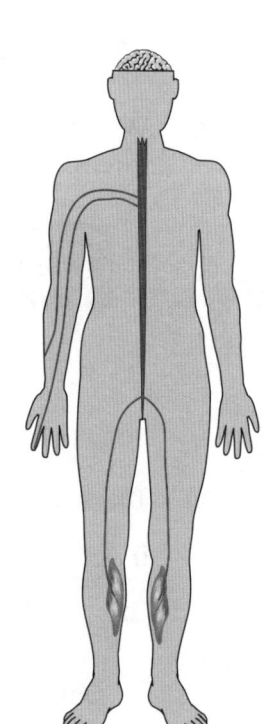

The Nervous System

Q4 The diagram below shows a typical **neurone**.

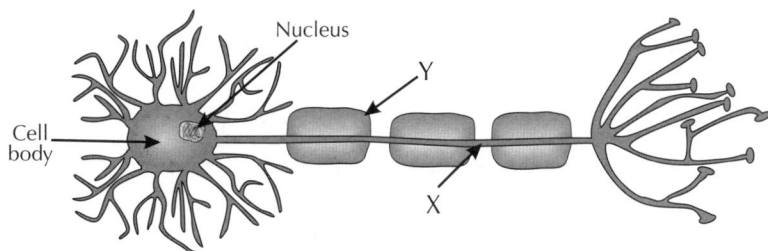

a) How does information travel along the neurone?

....

b) Complete the following sentences by circling the correct word in each pair.

> Structure X is the **synapse** / **axon** of the neurone. It's made from the neurone's **cytoplasm** / **nucleus** stretched into a long fibre and surrounded by a cell **membrane** / **wall**.

c) Name the part labelled **Y** and describe its function.

....

....

Q5 The neurones in the body **aren't directly connected** together — there are small **gaps** between them.

a) What **name** is given to the small gap between neurones?

....

b) Information is transmitted across the gap using **transmitter chemicals**. Explain how this works.

....

....

....

Q6 Some **drugs** affect **transmission** of impulses around the nervous system.

Describe an effect **ecstasy** (MDMA) has on the synapses in the brain and say why the drug is often described as having 'mood-enhancing effects'.

....

....

Module B6 — Brain and Mind

Reflexes

Q1 Circle the correct word(s) in each pair to complete the following sentences.

a) Reflexes happen more **quickly** / **slowly** than considered responses.

b) The neurones involved in reflexes go through the **back bone** / **spinal cord** or **an unconscious** / **a conscious** part of the brain.

c) Reflexes are **voluntary** / **involuntary**.

d) The main purpose of a reflex is to **protect** / **display** an organism.

e) The nervous pathway of a reflex is called a reflex **arc** / **ellipse**.

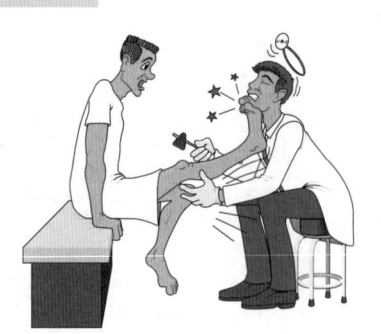

Q2 When you touch something **hot** with a finger you **automatically** pull the finger away. This is an example of a **reflex action**.

a) Complete the passage using words from the box below.

| motor   sensory   receptors   effector   relay   stimulus   CNS |

When the .... is detected by .... in the finger an impulse is sent along a .... neurone to the .... The impulse is then passed to a .... neurone. The impulse is relayed to a .... neurone, which carries the impulse to the ....

b) The diagram opposite shows some parts of the nervous system involved in a reflex action. Write the letter that shows:

   i) a relay neurone ....

   ii) a motor neurone ....

   iii) a sensory neurone ....

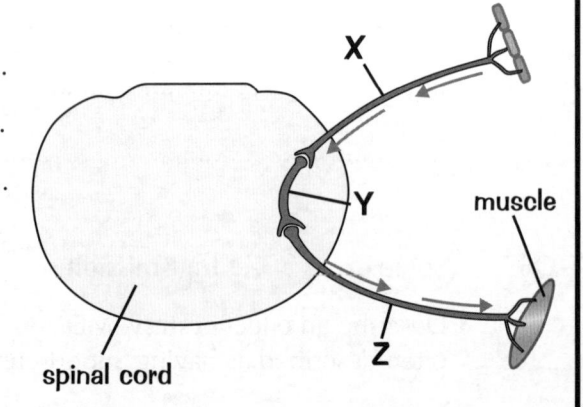

Top Tips:
Reflexes are really fast — that's the whole point of them. And the fewer synapses the signals have to cross, the faster the reaction. Doctors test people's reflexes by tapping below their knees to make their legs jerk. This reflex takes less than 50 milliseconds as only two synapse are involved.

Module B6 — Brain and Mind

Reflexes

Q3 **Earthworms** rely on **reflexes** for most of their behaviour. Give one **disadvantage** of this.

....

....

Q4 Draw lines to match the reflex with the way in which it **helps** the animal **survive**.

- a bird making its feathers stand on end
- a turtle retracting its head and limbs into its shell
- a jellyfish moving its tentacles when it senses movement
- a spider running onto its web when it feels it move
- a mollusc closing its shell

- finding food
- sheltering from a predator
- finding a mate

Q5 Look carefully at the diagrams showing two different **eyes** below.

Eye A   Eye B   pupil

a) Which diagram do you think shows an eye in **bright light**? Give a reason for your answer.

....

....

b) Is the response illustrated by the diagrams above a **considered** response or a **reflex** response?

....

c) Why is it an **advantage** to have this type of response controlling the action of the eye?

....

....

Module B6 — Brain and Mind

Learning and Modifying Reflexes

Q1 Read the passage about **Ivan Pavlov** and answer the questions that follow.

> Ivan Pavlov's most famous experiment looked at conditioning in dogs. The experiment was based on the observation that dogs salivated every time they smelt food. In his experiment a bell was rung just before the dogs were fed. Eventually he noticed that the dogs would salivate when the bell was rung even if they couldn't smell food.

a) From the passage, identify the:

   i) primary stimulus ....

   ii) secondary stimulus ....

   iii) unconditioned reflex ....

   iv) conditioned reflex ....

b) Which reflex, conditioned or unconditioned, has been learnt?

   ....

c) Complete the following sentence by circling the correct words.

> In a conditioned reflex the final response has **a direct connection** / **no direct connection** to the secondary stimulus.

Q2 Birds can **learn** to reject insects with certain colourings — this is a **conditioned reflex**.

a) Put the following statements in order to show how a conditioned reflex can increase a bird's chances of survival. The first one has been done for you.

   ☐ The bird spots a red coloured caterpillar and avoids it.

   ☐ The bird has increased its chances of survival by avoiding being poisoned.

   [1] A bird spots a red coloured caterpillar. It swoops down, catches and eats the caterpillar.

   ☐ The bird learns to associate feeling unwell with the bright colours.

   ☐ The bird feels unwell because of poisons in the insect.

b) In this example, what is the **primary** stimulus?

   ....

Q3 Give one example of when it would be useful to **modify** a reflex response and describe in terms of neurones how the reflex arc is modified.

....

....

Module B6 — Brain and Mind

Brain Development and Learning

Q1 Tick the boxes to show whether each statement is **true** or **false**.

		True	False
a)	The brain contains around one million neurones.	☐	☐
b)	Complex animals with a brain are able to learn by experience.	☐	☐
c)	The brain coordinates complex behaviour such as social behaviour.	☐	☐

Q2 Complete the passage using words from the box below.

> more   experience   unconnected   less   network
> stimulated   developed   trillions   formed

Most of the neurone connections in a newborn baby's brain are not yet ...., so the brain is only partly .... Every new .... causes the brain to become .... developed. When neurones in the brain are .... they branch out, forming connections between cells that were previously .... This forms a massive .... of neurones with .... of different routes for impulses to travel down.

Q3 Sarah and Sophie both play the **piano**. Sarah has been **practising** all week but Sophie **hasn't practised at all**. The girls' piano teacher, Mr Fudge, compliments Sarah on her performance but tells Sophie that he thinks she needs to practise more next week.

Explain why some skills can be **learnt** through **repetition**. Use diagrams to explain your answer.

....
....
....
....
....

Module B6 — Brain and Mind

Learning Skills and Behaviour

Q1 Explain why **complex animals**, such as humans, are able to **adapt** to new situations better than **simple animals**, such as insects.

....

....

Q2 Read the two case studies about **feral children** below and answer the questions that follow.

> Isabelle was discovered in 1938 at the age of about six. She'd spent most of her life locked in a darkened room with her mother who was deaf and unable to speak. Isabelle was unable to walk and she had the mental age of a nineteen-month old child. She rapidly learnt to speak and write. By the age of eight Isabelle had reached a 'normal' level and was eventually able to go to school, participating in all activities with other children.

> Eleven-year old Tissa was discovered in 1973 in Sri Lanka. When he was caught he showed many animal characteristics, such as walking on all fours, snarling at humans and yelping. Tissa was taken into care, and although he learned to smile and to eat with his hands, he never learned how to speak.

a) What is meant by the term '**critical period**'?

....

b) Do the case studies provide **evidence** of critical periods in child development? Explain your answer.

....

....

Q3 Hew has been in a **car accident**. Bruising on his **head** suggests that he took a nasty blow during the crash. The doctors are also concerned because he's having difficulty speaking and is unable to remember simple facts.

a) What part of Hew's **brain** might have been **damaged**?

....

b) Name **two** other things that this part of the brain is important for.

1. ....

2. ....

Top Tips: Language development isn't the only thing in humans with a critical period — binocular vision, balance and hearing do too. They don't just occur in humans either — e.g. some birds never learn the proper bird song for their species if they're kept in isolation when they're young.

Module B6 — Brain and Mind

Studying the Brain

Q1 Studying the brain can be useful for a number of reasons, for example in the **diagnosis** of people with brain disorders such as Parkinson's disease. Give **three methods** used by scientists to **map** the regions of the **cortex**.

1. ....
2. ....
3. ....

Q2 There are two main types of **memory** — **short-term** and **long-term**.

a) Where are the following memories likely to be stored? Put a letter **S** in the boxes next to any memories likely to be stored in **short-term** memory and a letter **L** in those likely to be stored in **long-term** memory.

- The rides you went on when you visited a theme park last month. ☐
- The smell of hot apple pie drifting through from the kitchen as it's being baked. ☐
- What you had for tea last Wednesday. ☐
- Something that happened in an episode of The Bill half an hour ago. ☐
- What your great aunt Gladys got you for your birthday when you were fourteen. ☐
- Answering a question in an exam about a topic you learnt two months ago. ☐

b) There are a number of things that can influence how humans remember information.

i) Jerry is trying to remember two phone numbers:

A. 01951 845217 and **B. 01234 543210**

Which number, A or B, is Jerry most likely to remember? Give a reason for your answer.

....

....

ii) If **strong stimuli** are associated with information it can help people remember more. Give **three** of these stimuli.

1. .... 2. .... 3. ....

iii) Give **one** other method used by humans to make them **more likely** to remember information.

....

Module B6 — Brain and Mind

Memory Mapping

Q1 Read the passage below and answer the questions that follow.

The ability to store information in our brains, for retrieval later on, is something that most of us take for granted. However, the mechanisms that underlie memory are not yet fully understood. What is known is that certain areas of the brain are crucial for memory processing. The discovery of some of these areas has come from attempts to treat people with epilepsy.

Epilepsy is a condition that causes sufferers to have repeated seizures. The cause of a seizure is not usually known, but they are always accompanied by a change in the electrical activity in the cerebral cortex of the brain. The abnormal electrical activity tends to start in an area where the neurones are highly sensitive, and then spread out across the cortex. Epileptic seizures can often be controlled using anticonvulsant drugs, and sometimes with surgery.

Between the 1930s and 1950s, Wilder Penfield investigated the areas of his patients' brains that were prone to seizures using electrical stimulation. By systematically stimulating points in the cortex, Penfield was able to determine the link between certain areas and their functions. For example, when he stimulated a particular area patients would feel tingling sensations in their skin, showing that this area was involved in the sense of touch. When he stimulated a region of the brain called the temporal lobe (shown in the diagram) some of his patients seemed to experience memories of past events — suggesting that the temporal lobe is part of the system for recalling stored memories.

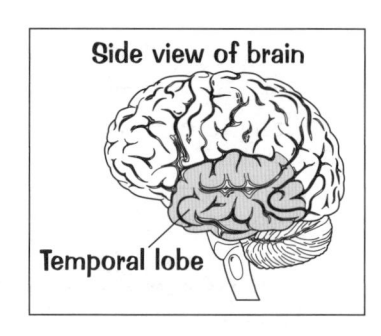

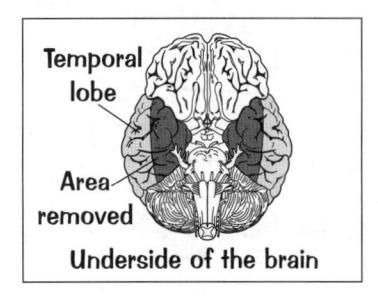

Further evidence for the involvement of the temporal lobe in memory came from a patient who was given surgery for his epilepsy in 1953. The patient, known as H.M., had part of the temporal lobe on both sides of his brain removed to try to control his seizures. The diagram shows the areas removed.

The operation was successful, in that H.M.'s seizures were reduced, but it left him with severe amnesia (memory loss). The interesting thing about H.M.'s amnesia was that it was very selective. H.M. can remember the experiences of his childhood, showing that his long-term memories stored before the operation were not affected. He is also able to learn new tasks and retain details of what he is doing, showing that his short-term memory still works. However, what H.M. can't do is form any new long-term memories. For example, the doctor who has worked with H.M. for over 40 years since the operation has to reintroduce herself every time they meet — H.M. has no memory of who she is.

Since the case of H.M. doctors have investigated other ways to map the areas of a patient's brain involved in memory. One method currently used is to take MRI scans of a patient's brain while they are performing memory tasks. MRI scans use a strong magnetic field to monitor changes in the blood flow around the brain and highlight areas of high activity. The theory is that by working out the areas that are active during the memory tasks, the scientist can determine which areas are needed for memory processing.

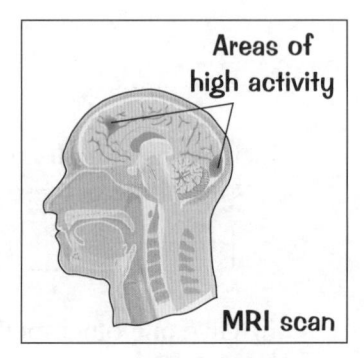

It is hoped that in the future a model will be devised that fully explains how our brains process memories — until then it remains an ongoing area of research.

Module B6 — Brain and Mind

Memory Mapping

a) Complete the definition of memory by filling in the blanks.

> Memory is the .... and .... of information.

b) Briefly describe how each of the methods described in the article was useful in determining the areas of the brain associated with memory:

   i) Electrical stimulation. ....

   ....

   ii) Study of H.M. ....

   ....

   iii) MRI scans during memory tasks. ....

   ....

c) What **type** of memory was recalled when Penfield stimulated the temporal lobe?
Circle the correct answer.

   long-term memory   **short-term memory**   **mid-term memory**

d) Why was the patient H.M. so useful in determining the function of certain brain areas?

   ....

e) Describe which parts of H.M.'s memory were:

   i) **Unaffected** by his operation.

   ....

   ....

   ii) **Damaged** by his operation.

   ....

   ....

f) Why is the study of memory an ongoing area of research?

   ....

   ....

   ....

H.M.'s memory is an ongoing area of research, and an important tourist attraction.

Module B6 — Brain and Mind

Respiration

Q1 Tick the correct boxes to show whether the sentences are **true** or **false**.

True False

a) Respiration releases energy from food. ☐ ☐
b) Respiration usually releases energy from protein. ☐ ☐
c) Aerobic respiration is more efficient than anaerobic respiration. ☐ ☐
d) Aerobic respiration requires oxygen. ☐ ☐
e) Breathing is a kind of respiration. ☐ ☐

Q2 Use the words given to complete the word equations for the **two types** of respiration. Each word can be used more than once.

carbon dioxide   oxygen   lactic acid   water   glucose   energy

Aerobic: .... + ... → .... + ... (+ ....)

Anaerobic: .... → .... (+ ....)

Q3 Use the words below to fill in the blanks and complete the following paragraph.

released   used   synthesise   glucose   required   ATP   energy currency   break down
Energy .... by respiration is used to .... a small molecule called .... This molecule is the .... of living things.

Q4 Complete the following sentences by circling the correct answers.

a) During exercise our muscles need more **energy / water**, which they get from **oxygen / ATP**, to enable them to keep contracting.

b) This means they need a continuous supply of **protein / glucose** and **carbon dioxide / oxygen**.

c) Extra oxygen is obtained and the extra **carbon dioxide / glucose** is removed, by increasing the **breathing rate / rate of digestion**.

d) The heart rate **slows down / speeds up** to supply blood more **quickly / slowly** to the muscles.

e) Eventually the muscles become **tired / energised**, particularly when energy is released **with / without** oxygen (**anaerobic / aerobic** respiration).

Respiration

Q5 Jim is a keen runner. He takes part in a 400 metre race. The **graph** below shows Jim's **breathing rate** before, during and after the race.

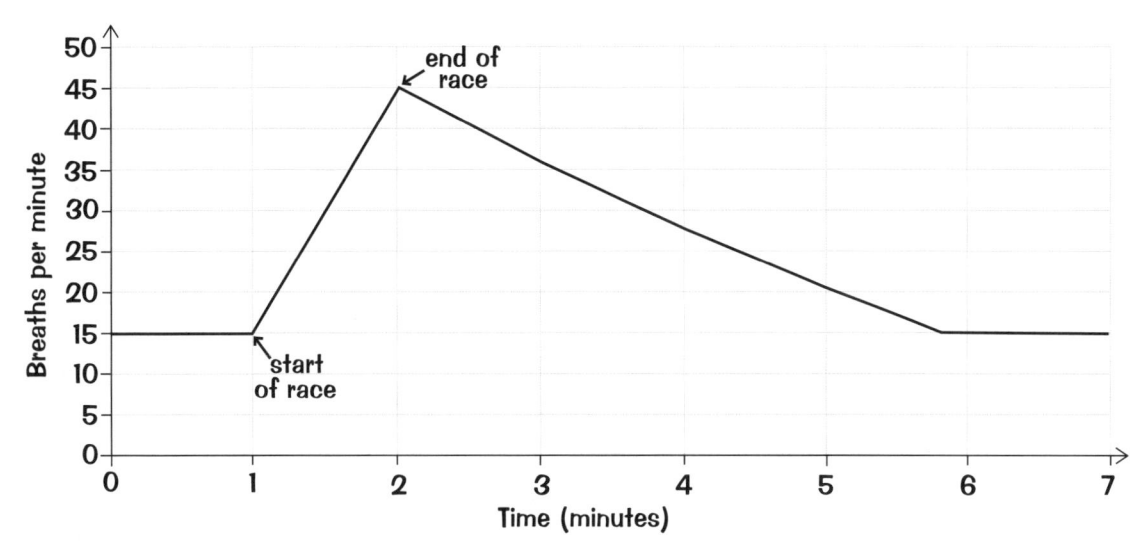

a) How much does Jim's breathing rate go up during the race?

.... **breaths per minute**

b) What product of anaerobic respiration builds up in the muscles during exercise?

....

c) Why **doesn't** Jim's breathing rate return to normal immediately after the race?

Think about the answer to part b).

....

....

....

Q6 Amy used a **digital monitor** to measure how her body changed during exercise.

a) What **two** things could Amy monitor?

1. ....

2. ....

b) Amy wants to know if her measurements are normal so she records them and takes them to her doctor. Circle the correct words to complete the sentence below.

Amy's doctor tells her the normal levels of the measurements she has taken are

given as **an exact value / a range of values** and they vary between **individuals / twins**.

Module B7 — Further Biology

Blood and Blood Typing

Q1 Blood is made up of four components.

a) Circle the **four** components of blood.

microbes   clear blood cells   red blood cells   plasma   white blood cells   platelets   nucleus

b) Tick the boxes to show whether the statements are true or false.

		True	False
i)	The function of red blood cells is to fight germs.	☐	☐
ii)	White blood cells help to clot blood.	☐	☐
iii)	Red blood cells carry oxygen.	☐	☐
iv)	The liquid part of blood is called urine.	☐	☐
v)	Platelets help to seal wounds to prevent blood loss.	☐	☐

Q2 There are four different **blood types** or **groups**, which are represented by letters.

a) Name the **four** blood types.

1. ....   2. ....

3. ....   4. ....

b) What do the letters refer to? ....

c) Where in the blood are **antibodies** found?
Tick the correct answer.

☐ On red blood cells   ☐ In the plasma

☐ On white blood cells   ☐ On the platelets

d) Where in the blood are the **antigens** that determine blood type found? Tick the correct answer.

☐ On red blood cells   ☐ In the plasma

☐ On white blood cells   ☐ On the platelets

Module B7 — Further Biology

Blood and Blood Typing

Q3 Complete the table below to show the correct **antigens** and **antibodies** for each blood type.

Blood type	Antigens present	Antibodies present
		anti-B
	B	
AB		
	none	

Q4 The presence or absence of blood type antigens determines who can receive **blood transfusions** from certain donors.

a) In what situation might you need a blood transfusion?

....

b) Tick the correct answer to show whether a person can **receive** or **donate** a particular blood type.

    Yes   No

   i) If they are blood type **A**, can they **receive** blood type **B**?   ☐ ☐

   ii) If they are blood type **A**, can they **receive** blood type **O**?   ☐ ☐

   iii) If they are blood type **AB**, can they **receive** blood type **B**?   ☐ ☐

   iv) If they are blood type **AB**, can they **donate** to blood type **B**?   ☐ ☐

Use the table you have just filled in to help you.

c) Which blood type can **donate** their blood to **any** other blood type? ....

d) Which blood type can only **receive** blood of the **same** blood type? ....

e) Explain why a person with blood type A can't accept blood from a person with blood type B.

....

....

Top Tips: You might be asked to interpret data on blood transfusions in the exam. If you do, don't panic — think about the antigens and antibodies present and draw a table if it helps you.

Module B7 — Further Biology

Inheritance of Blood Types

Q1 a) What are **alleles**?

....

b) Draw lines to link the type of allele with its description.

Dominant — You need two copies of this type of allele for an organism to display the characteristic of the allele.

Recessive — If you have two different alleles for a certain characteristic, the version of the characteristic that appears is caused by this type of allele.

Q2 Blood type depends on which alleles you **inherit** from your **parents**.

Fill in the blanks with the words given to complete the paragraph on inheritance of blood types.

six   recessive   three   blood type   co-dominant   antigens   genotype   genes   antibodies   AB   phenotype   A

Some .... have more than two alleles. ABO .... is determined by a single gene with .... alleles. The alleles for type A and B are .... This means the .... is a mix of the characteristics from both alleles. If you had an A and a B allele your blood type would be .... and you would have both A and B .... on the surface of your red blood cells.

Q3 There are **four** different **blood types** because of the combination of **three different alleles**.

Complete the table below to show the four possible blood types and their alleles. One has been done for you.

Remember, I^O is recessive.

Blood type	Alleles
A	or $I^A I^O$
B	or
AB	
O	

I^A = Allele for A
I^B = Allele for B
I^O = Allele for O

Module B7 — Further Biology

Inheritance of Blood Types

Q4 A woman with blood type alleles $I^A I^A$ and a man with blood type alleles $I^B I^B$ are trying to work out the possible blood types of their children.

a) What blood type is:

i) the man? ....

ii) the woman? ....

Use the table you filled in on the previous page to help you.

b) Complete the genetic diagram to show the possible combinations of alleles in their children.

Parents: female $I^A I^A$ — male $I^B I^B$

Gametes:

Children:

c) Circle the possible blood type(s) of their children.

Blood type AB   **Blood type O**   **Blood type B**   **Blood type A**

Q5 Here is another genetic diagram showing the inheritance of blood types.

a) Complete the diagram.

Parents: female — male

Gametes: I^A I^O I^B I^O

Children:

b) What blood type is:

i) the female? ....

ii) the male? ....

c) List the possible blood type(s) of the children.

....

Module B7 — Further Biology

The Circulatory System

Q1 The diagram below shows the human **heart**, as seen from the front. The left atrium has been labelled. Complete the remaining labels a) to j).

a) ....

b) ....

c) ....

d) ....

e) ....

f) ....

g) ....

left atrium

h) ....

i) ....

j) ....

k) What is the function of the valves in the heart and in veins?

....

l) Use the words given to fill in the blanks in the paragraph below.

| vein | heart | deoxygenated | lungs | artery | oxygenated | double |

Humans have a .... circulatory system. In the first circuit, blood is pumped from the .... to the .... In the second circuit, ... blood leaves the heart and goes around to body and .... blood returns to the heart.

Q2 Tick the boxes below to say whether each statement is **true** or **false**.

		True	False
a)	Arteries are tiny blood vessels.	☐	☐
b)	As blood passes through capillary beds small molecules are forced out of the capillaries to form the tissue fluid.	☐	☐
c)	Tissue fluid aids in the diffusion of chemicals between the capillaries and tissue.	☐	☐
d)	Waste chemicals like oxygen and glucose diffuse out of cells into tissue fluid.	☐	☐

Top Tips: When doctors use a stethoscope to listen to your heart, it's actually the valves closing that they hear. Make sure you understand why there are valves in the heart and veins.

Module B7 — Further Biology

The Skeletal System

Q1 Vertebrates have an **internal skeleton**.

a) Give **two** functions of a skeleton.

1. .... 2. ....

b) **Joints** allow the bones of the skeleton to move. Complete the labels i) to v).

i) ....

ii) ....

iii) ....

iv) ....

v) ....

c) Circle the correct words to complete the following sentences.

> **Cartilage / A ligament** acts like a shock absorber at the joint, preventing the **muscles / bones** rubbing together. The synovial **membrane / fluid** is an oily substance which **lubricates / heats** the joint, allowing it to move more easily.

Q2 **Muscles** often work in **pairs**.

a) In the diagram, which muscle is **contracted** and which is **relaxed**? Tick the correct boxes.

	Contracted	Relaxed
Biceps	☐	☐
Triceps	☐	☐

b) Circle the correct word from each pair to complete the passage below.

> Muscles can only pull. To make a joint move you need **two / three** muscles that can pull in **opposite directions / the same direction**. **Agonistic / Antagonistic** muscles are pairs of muscles that work against each other. When one muscle contracts (**shortens / lengthens**) the other relaxes (**shortens / lengthens**).

Module B7 — Further Biology

Health and Fitness

Q1 Health and fitness practitioners **monitor** their patients and clients **closely** during and after treatments and training programmes.

    a) Give two reasons why a **health** practitioner would monitor a patient.

        1. ....

        2. ....

    b) Give two reasons why a **fitness** practitioner would monitor a client.

        1. ....

        2. ....

Q2 Grania has gone to see her **doctor** about a nasty **cold** she has had for a few weeks. The doctor asks Grania some questions.

    a) Circle the useful question(s) the doctor may have asked Grania.

- Do you smoke?
- How many brothers or sisters do you have?
- Have you had a cold like this before?
- What are your symptoms?
- How many GCSEs do you have?

    b) Why might the doctor ask Grania about her **family medical history**?

        ....

    c) The doctor takes lots of **notes**. Why do practitioners do this?
Tick the boxes to show whether the following statements are true or false.

Statement	True	False
So they can share the information with other members of their team.	☐	☐
So they can share the information with the surgery cleaner.	☐	☐
So they can remember the details of each patient.	☐	☐
So they can pass on the information to pharmaceutical companies.	☐	☐
So they can monitor changes in the patient's condition.	☐	☐

Module B7 — Further Biology

Health and Fitness

Q3 Trevor has had a tickly cough since he began taking tablets for high blood pressure. His doctor has told him to keep taking the tablets.

a) Why would a doctor suggest taking a treatment even when there are **side effects**?
....

b) The cough gets worse and Trevor can no longer work as an opera singer. Trevor's doctor **modifies** his treatment.
Fill in the blanks in the passage using the words given below.

damage	modify	side effects	benefits	improvements
Trevor's doctor modified his treatment because the .... outweighed the .... Practitioners may also .... a treatment or programme if it's causing .... or not producing any ....

Q4 Different treatment and fitness programmes will have different **targets**.

a) Suggest two general targets.

1. ....

2. ....

b) After a target has been reached, why should monitoring **continue**?
....

Q5 Practitioners need to assess their clients' progress, which depends upon the **accuracy** and **reliability** of the monitoring system.

Write a brief explanation of the terms accuracy and reliability including the words given below.

results   consistent   close   actual value

a) Accuracy ....
....

b) Reliability ....
....

Module B7 — Further Biology

Health and Fitness

Q6 **Excessive exercise** can cause **injuries**.

Write a short description of each of the common injuries given below.

a) A sprain ....

b) A dislocation ....

Q7 a) List the two main **symptoms** of a **sprain**.

1. ....

2. ....

b) What is the **name** of the method used to treat a sprain? ....

c) Complete the following sentences on the treatment of a sprain, using the words given below.

bandage   rest   elevation   raising   damage   reduce   ice   compression
• .... — to avoid any further .... • .... — applied to the area to help .... swelling. • .... — a .... is placed around the injured part. • .... — involves .... the injured limb to reduce swelling.

Q8 Some injuries caused by excessive exercise may require **special care**.

Circle the correct word(s) from each pair to complete the following paragraph.

> More serious injuries may be treated by a **physiotherapist / psychologist**, who specialises in injuries of the **cardiovascular / skeletal-muscular** system. They will **give treatment / do surgery** to reduce swelling and pain, and give therapies to **slow down / speed up** healing. They will also advise on the best **clothing / exercises** to help **rehabilitate / cure** the affected area.

Module B7 — Further Biology

Blood Transfusions

Q1 Read the following passage about **blood transfusions**.

Blood Transfusions

8,000 units of blood products are used each day in the United Kingdom, but of the people who can donate, only 5% (1.6 million people) actually do so. Last year 2.1 million units of blood were collected in the UK. The increasing numbers of people requiring blood transfusions and the decreasing numbers of donors are leading to a national blood shortage. But it's not just the lack of donors that causes problems in blood transfusion:

- There are four types of blood group in humans, linked to the type of antigens found on the surface of red blood cells — types A, B, AB and O. Because of these antigens people must have their blood type checked and matched with a suitable type of donated blood before receiving a transfusion.

- Donated blood has a shelf-life of 35 days and it's expensive — around £120 for one unit to be collected, tested, stored and distributed.

- There have been problems, especially in recent years, from blood transfusions involving donated blood contaminated with diseases such as HIV and CJD.

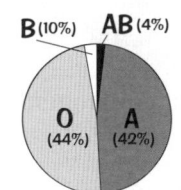

Percentage of UK population with each blood type: B (10%), AB (4%), O (44%), A (42%)

The blood shortage is at crisis point. Lots of time and money are being used in national schemes to promote blood donation and in scientific research to find alternative ways of reducing the shortage:

Artificial Blood

Some scientists are looking for possible replacements for real blood. Their aim is to make a replacement oxygen carrier that could be dehydrated, then stored for long periods of time and rehydrated to use when needed. As the blood would be artificially created, the chances of contamination would be massively reduced and large-scale production would result in a lower price per unit.

Altered Blood

Recently a group of scientists has managed to 'convert' A, B and AB type blood into O type blood. The group isolated an enzyme from bacteria that can chop off the sugar groups found on the surface of A, B and AB type red blood cells. If used in a clinical setting this could stop the need for blood testing before transfusions, reduce the number of cases of transfusion of the wrong blood type and help to ease the blood shortage crisis.

Module B7 — Further Biology

Blood Transfusions

a) What percentage of the UK population that can donate blood actually do so? ....

b) What percentage of the UK population can **receive only** type **O** blood? Circle the correct answer.

    42%   44%   10%   4%

c) i) List **three** advantages of using 'artificial' blood over using real blood.

1. ....

2. ....

3. ....

ii) What **component** of the blood would 'artificial' blood replace?

The aim is to make a replacement oxygen carrier.

....

d) i) List **two** advantages of 'altered' blood.

1. ....

2. ....

ii) Why is it beneficial to be able to turn type A, B and AB blood into O type blood?

....

e) What type of molecule are the **sugar groups** removed from the A, B and AB red blood cells? Tick the one correct answer.

☐ antibodies
☐ antigens
☐ microbes
☐ platelets

f) If a patient with type **A** blood **received** a transfusion of blood type **AB**, what would happen to their blood?

....

Module B7 — Further Biology

Pyramids of Numbers and Biomass

Q1 Complete the passage below by circling the correct words.

As you move up trophic levels, the organisms are usually **greater** / **fewer** in number, the amount of biomass **increases** / **decreases**, and there is a **rise** / **fall** in the amount of energy available.

Q2 **Tick** the correct columns to show which of the following are features of pyramids of **numbers** and which are features of pyramids of **biomass**. For each feature you might need to tick **one** column, **both**, or **neither**.

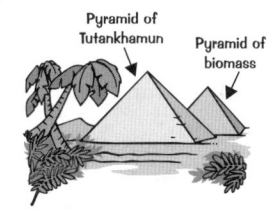

Feature	Pyramid of numbers	Pyramid of biomass
Mass of organisms represented at each level.		
Each bar represents a step in a food chain.		
Always starts with a producer.		
Numbers are represented at each step.		

Q3 Diagrams **A**, **B**, **C**, **D** and **E** show some **pyramids of numbers** and **pyramids of biomass** based on data collected from Farmer MacDonald's land.

a) Which of the pyramids could be pyramids of numbers? ....

b) Which of the pyramids could be pyramids of biomass? Explain your answer.

....

....

c) Which of the pyramids could be a pyramid of numbers representing the following food chains?

i) Oak tree → caterpillars → blackbirds → buzzards ....

ii) Dandelions → snails → hedgehogs → fleas ....

d) Give one advantage of pyramids of numbers and one advantage of pyramids of biomass.

....

....

Top Tips: Pyramids of numbers are not always pyramid shapes, which can be a little confusing... but 'wonky shapes of numbers' doesn't quite have the same ring to it really, does it? Pyramids of biomass are the ones that very nearly always come out as nice pyramid shapes.

Module B7 — Further Biology

Energy Transfer and Energy Flow

Q1 Complete the sentences below by circling the correct words.

a) Nearly all life on Earth depends on **food** / **energy** from the Sun.

b) **Heterotrophs** / **Autotrophs** obtain their energy by eating other organisms.

c) **Plants** / **Animals** can make their own food by a process called **photosynthesis** / **respiration**.

d) To obtain energy animals must **decay** / **eat** plant material or other animals.

e) Animals and plants release energy through the process of **photosynthesis** / **respiration**.

f) Some of the energy released in animals is **gained** / **lost** through **growth** / **movement** (and in many other ways) before it reaches organisms at later steps of the food chain.

g) Organisms that are able to produce their own food are called **heterotrophs** / **autotrophs**.

Q2 A **food chain** is shown in the diagram.

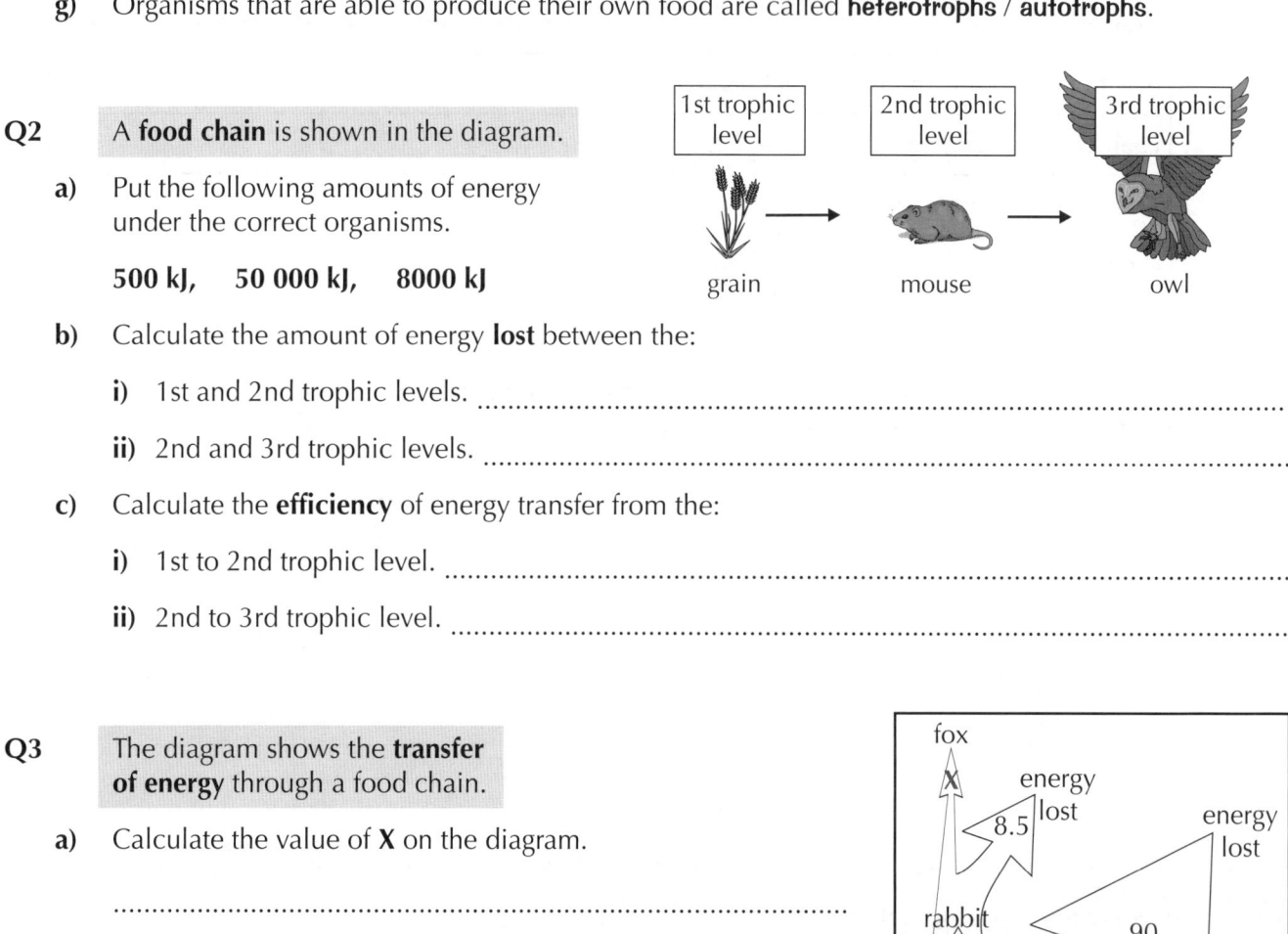

a) Put the following amounts of energy under the correct organisms.

500 kJ, 50 000 kJ, 8000 kJ

b) Calculate the amount of energy **lost** between the:

i) 1st and 2nd trophic levels. ....

ii) 2nd and 3rd trophic levels. ....

c) Calculate the **efficiency** of energy transfer from the:

i) 1st to 2nd trophic level. ....

ii) 2nd to 3rd trophic level. ....

Q3 The diagram shows the **transfer of energy** through a food chain.

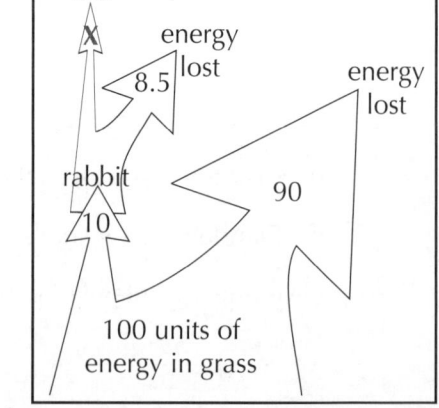

a) Calculate the value of **X** on the diagram.

....

b) Calculate the percentage of energy from the **grass** that is obtained by the **fox**.

....

c) Describe **two** ways in which energy can be lost from a food chain.

....
....
....

Module B7 — Further Biology

Energy Transfer and Energy Flow

Q4 Another **food chain** is shown below.

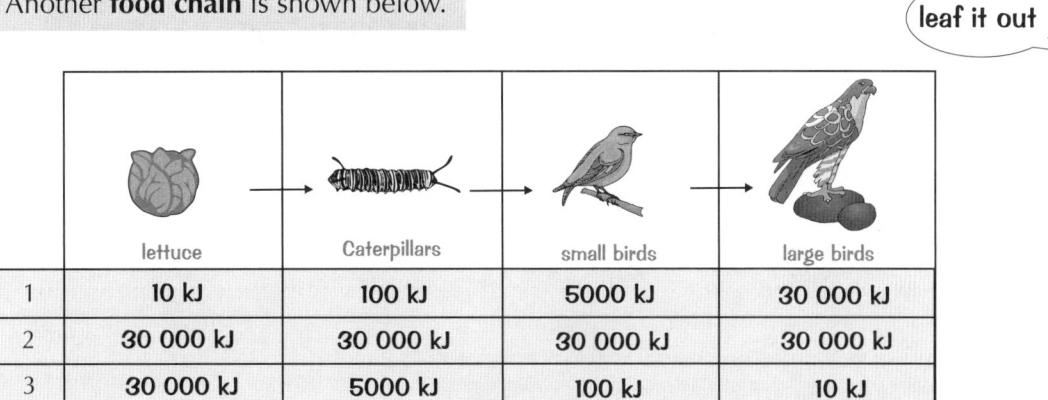

	lettuce	Caterpillars	small birds	large birds
1	10 kJ	100 kJ	5000 kJ	30 000 kJ
2	30 000 kJ	30 000 kJ	30 000 kJ	30 000 kJ
3	30 000 kJ	5000 kJ	100 kJ	10 kJ

a) Which row, 1, 2 or 3, shows the amount of energy available at each trophic level? ....

b) Circle the answer below that shows how much energy is available to the **caterpillars**.

   5000 kJ   25 000 kJ   30 000 kJ

c) Why do food chains rarely have more than five trophic levels?

   ....

   ....

Q5 An **aquatic food chain** is shown below.

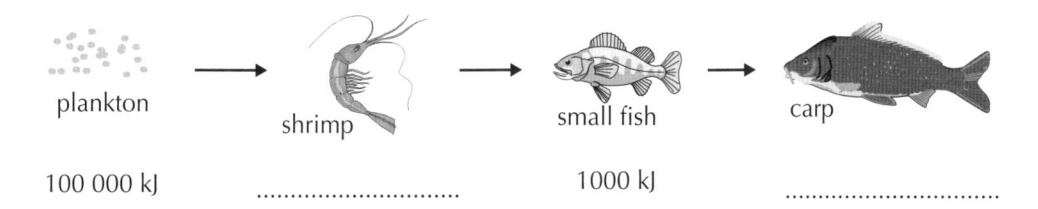

plankton → shrimp → small fish → carp

100 000 kJ   ....   1000 kJ   ....

a) 90 000 kJ is lost between the 1st trophic level (plankton) and the 2nd trophic level (shrimp).

   i) On the diagram, write the amount of energy available in the **shrimp** for the **small fish**.

   ii) Calculate the **efficiency** of energy transfer from the 1st to the 2nd trophic level.

   ....

b) The energy transfer from the small fish to the carp is **5%** efficient.

   i) On the diagram, write the amount of **energy** available in the **carp**.

   ii) How much energy is **lost** from the food chain at this stage?

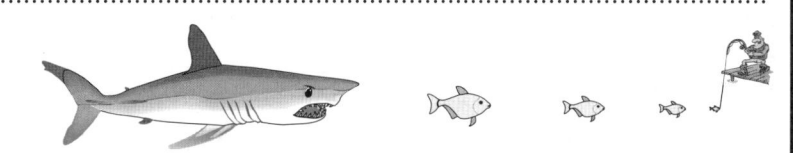

   ....

Module B7 — Further Biology

Biomass in Soil

Q1 Soil is made up of **four main components**, including water and biomass.

Describe the other **two** components of soil.

....

....

....

Q2 Sue is a farmer. She wants to know what **percentage** of the **soil** is **water** in each of her **three fields**.

Sue collects soil samples from each field and heats them, evaporating off all the water. A dish with a mass of **50 g** was used to weigh the soil. Her results are shown below.

	Mass of soil + dish before heating (g)	Mass of soil + dish after heating (g)
Field A	205	175
Field B	190	160
Field C	200	180

a) Calculate the percentage of water in the soil from field **C**.

....

b) Why is it important to know how much the dish weighs?

....

c) Which soil sample has the **highest** percentage of water?

....

....

....

d) Suggest why farmers might want to know the amount of water in their soil.

....

Top Tips: You need to be able to calculate the amount of water and biomass in a sample of soil. It's pretty easy once you know how, and this percentage calculation is really handy. You could use it to work out other exciting things, like the percentage of time you spend revising... actually don't.

Module B7 — Further Biology

Biomass in Soil

Q3 There are simple procedures you can carry out to find the amount of water and biomass in soil.

a) Number the boxes to show how the amount of water in soil can be measured.

☐ The previous three steps are repeated until the mass stays constant.

☐ The soil is heated in an oven at a temperature between 90 and 110 °C.

☐ The soil is left to cool.

☐ Soil is collected and weighed.

☐ A percentage is calculated.

☐ The soil is weighed.

b) Briefly explain the procedure you would use to determine the amount of **biomass** in soil once the water had been removed.

....

....

Q4 Andy is looking for an allotment to grow his own vegetables.
He decides to measure the amount of **biomass** in the soil at several sites.

a) Andy collects one soil sample from each site. Explain whether this would give him an accurate percentage of biomass on each allotment.

....

....

b) At one site Andy found that the percentage of biomass in the soil was **30%**.
He decides to collect another sample of **100 g** from the same site.
How many grams of biomass would you expect there to be in the sample?

....

c) Do you think Andy would prefer an allotment with a high or low percentage of biomass? Give a reason for your answer.

....

....

Module B7 — Further Biology

Symbiosis

Q1 Parasitism and commensalism are both types of symbiosis.

a) What is meant by the term symbiosis?

....

b) In a parasitic relationship one organism benefits.
What is the name given to the other organism in the relationship.

....

c) Put a tick in the box next to the statement that correctly describes commensalism.

☐ one organism benefits and the other is neither helped nor harmed

☐ one organism benefits and the other is harmed

☐ both organisms benefit from the relationship

Q2 Describe two ways parasites have an impact on humans.

1. ....

2. ....

Q3 Parasites have special features that help them to survive in their environment.

a) Name two parasites.

1. ....

2. ....

b) Explain how the features of one of these parasites enables it to be successful.

....

....

....

Q4 Explain why the evolution of a parasite is closely linked to that of its host.

....

....

Module B7 — Further Biology

Parasitism

Q1 **Sickle-cell anaemia** is a **recessive genetic disorder** which affects the **red blood cells**. The recessive allele for sickle-cell anaemia is **a**, and the dominant allele is **A**.

a) Give **two symptoms** of sickle-cell anaemia.

1. .... 2. ....

b) What combination of alleles is possessed by:

i) a **carrier** for sickle-cell anaemia.   ....

ii) a **sufferer** of sickle-cell anaemia.   ....

iii) an **unaffected** person (who is not a carrier).   ....

c) Dave and Jane are both carriers of the sickle-cell anaemia allele. **Complete** the following genetic diagram to show the possible inheritance of the allele, if Dave and Jane have children together.

Jane (Aa)   Dave (Aa)

Gametes:

Possible offspring:

d) i) Based on the diagram, what is the probability of a child being a **carrier** of the sickle-cell allele (but not having the disease)?

....

ii) Briefly describe why carriers of the sickle-cell allele have some protection from **malaria**.

....

....

Q2 In places where **malaria** is common the sickle-cell allele has become frequent in the population.

Number the boxes to show how **natural selection** has increased the frequency of sickle-cell anaemia.

☐ A carrier of the sickle-cell allele is less likely to die of malaria.

☐ The sickle-cell allele is produced by a mutation in DNA.

☐ The sickle-cell allele becomes more frequent in the population.

☐ The carrier reproduces, passing on the sickle-cell allele.

Module B7 — Further Biology

Parasitism

Q3 Read the following passage about **parasitism** and then answer the questions that follow.

African Trypanosomes

Parasitic microorganisms called trypanosomes can cause disease in both humans and livestock. They cause African trypanosomiasis (more commonly called African sleeping sickness) in humans and nagana in livestock. These parasites have a major impact on public health and cause huge economic losses.

African sleeping sickness alone threatens over 60 million people in 36 countries of sub-Saharan Africa. In the early stages of the disease, symptoms include fever, headaches, pains in joints and itching. When the parasite infests the central nervous system the symptoms become more severe; they include a disturbance of the sleep cycle, confusion, sensory disturbances and poor coordination. It is thought that there are 300 000 new cases each year worldwide. However, less than 4 million people are being monitored and only about 40 000 are diagnosed and treated each year. Without treatment with drugs, the disease is fatal.

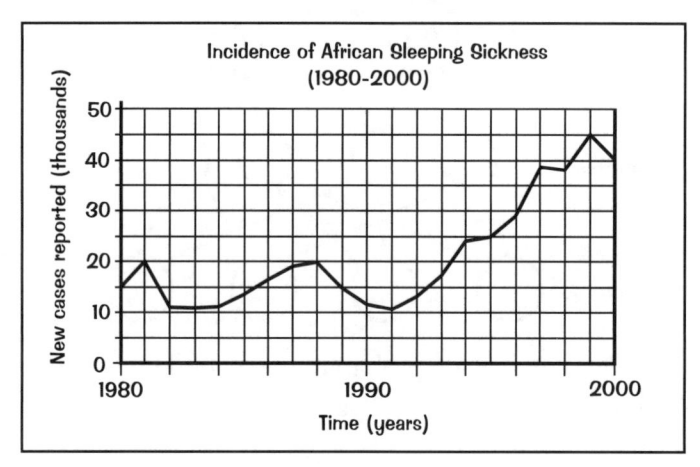

Incidence of African Sleeping Sickness (1980-2000)

These parasites can be transmitted by an insect — the tsetse fly. If a tsetse fly bites an infected animal it can take up the microorganism, which can then be transmitted to the tsetse's next victim. The distribution of African sleeping sickness throughout the world is closely linked to that of the tsetse fly.

The number of cases of African sleeping sickness has increased significantly since the 1980s, as shown in the graph above. It is thought that this is due to several factors, including inadequate drugs, insect control and monitoring. Control measures have broken down in some countries due to civil war and unrest, which may have caused an increase in cases.

The parasite is able to vary the proteins displayed on its surface when it is within a host. This allows the trypanosome to avoid being recognised by the mammal's immune system. This has made it hard for scientists to develop a vaccine against African sleeping sickness.

Nagana is also common in some African countries. It mainly affects cattle and horses. It causes an estimated economic loss of US $4.5 billion every year. This disease causes fever, and anaemia that leads to weakness, tiredness and weight loss. Some types of animal will die from nagana if they are not treated. Nagana in livestock is thought to be a major factor contributing to rural poverty in Africa as it can severely limit meat and dairy production and can prevent the use of oxen for ploughing.

Module B7 — Further Biology

Parasitism

a) Name two organisms that can act as hosts for trypanosomes.

1. ....

2. ....

b) State the approximate number of new reported cases of African sleeping sickness in **1990**.

....

c) Tick the statements below which can be concluded from the graph.

☐ More people are receiving treatment for African sleeping sickness.

☐ The number of people reported to be infected with African sleeping sickness each year has increased between 1980 and 2000.

☐ More children were infected with African sleeping sickness in 2000 than in 1980.

☐ The number of deaths from African sleeping sickness has increased.

d) Describe two **symptoms** of African sleeping sickness.

1. ....

2. ....

e) Approximately what percentage of new cases of African sleeping sickness are actually **diagnosed** and **treated**? Circle the correct answer.

3%   20%   13%   43%   50%

f) Explain why nagana causes huge **economic loss**.

....

....

g) Describe a **feature** of trypanosomes and explain how it helps them to be successful.

....

....

....

Top Tips: An increase in African sleeping sickness is great news for the trypanosomes, but very bad news for everyone else. This kind of relationship is the same for all parasites — one species thrives while another is harmed.

Module B7 — Further Biology

Photosynthesis

Q1 **Photosynthesis** is the process that produces 'food' in plants.

a) Use some of the words below to complete the equation for photosynthesis.

oxygen   carbon dioxide   nitrogen   water   glucose   sodium chloride

.... + ... —light energy→ .... + ...

b) Draw lines to match each word below to its correct description.

- chloroplast — a green pigment needed for photosynthesis
- chlorophyll — the food that is produced by photosynthesis
- sunlight — the structure in a cell where photosynthesis occurs
- glucose — supplies the energy for photosynthesis

Q2 Complete the passage using the words from the list below.

| convert | fruits | oxygen | leaves | cells | energy |

Plants make glucose in their .... Some of it is used for respiration, which releases .... The plant then uses some of this to .... the rest of the glucose into other substances for storage and to build new ....

Q3 The **glucose** made by photosynthesis has many different uses. The energy released from glucose can be used to make polymers that the plant needs.

a) i) What is glucose turned into in order to be stored in **roots**, **stems** and **leaves**?
....

ii) Why is this substance more suitable for storage than glucose?
....

b) What substances, used to make **proteins**, do plants collect from the soil?
....

c) What substance is glucose converted into in order to make **cell walls**?
....

Top Tips: It's really essential that you understand photosynthesis and learn what is needed for the process to work. Make sure you learn the different kinds of polymers that are made using the products of photosynthesis — they allow plants to grow and survive.

Module B7 — Further Biology

Rate of Photosynthesis

Q1 Define the term **'limiting factor'**.

....

....

Q2 Seth investigated the effect of different concentrations of **carbon dioxide** on the rate of photosynthesis of his Swiss cheese plant. He measured the rate of photosynthesis with increasing light intensity at **three** different CO_2 concentrations. The results are shown on the graph below.

a) What effect does increasing the concentration of CO_2 have on the rate of photosynthesis? Use the graph and your own knowledge.

....

....

....

b) Explain why all the lines level off eventually.

Think about the third limiting factor.

....

....

Q3 Lucy investigated the **volume of oxygen** produced by pondweed at **different intensities of light**. Her results are shown in the table below.

Relative light intensity	1	2	3	4	5
Volume of oxygen produced in 10 minutes (ml)	12	25	37	48	61

a) What was Lucy using the volume of oxygen produced as a measure of?

....

b) Plot a graph of her results.

c) Describe the relationship shown on the graph between light intensity and photosynthesis rate.

....

....

....

....

d) Would you expect this relationship to continue if Lucy continued to increase the light intensity? Explain your answer.

....

....

Module B7 — Further Biology

Rate of Photosynthesis

Q4 The rate of photosynthesis in some pondweed was recorded by counting the bubbles produced per minute at equal intervals during the day.

No. bubbles per minute	Time of day
0	06.00
10	12.00
20	18.00
0	

a) The time for the final reading is missing. Predict what the time is likely to be.

....

b) Explain why the rate of photosynthesis is 0 bubbles per minute for this time of day.

....

c) Suggest where plants get their food from at this time of day.

....

d) Plot a **bar graph** on the grid on the right to display the results shown in the table.

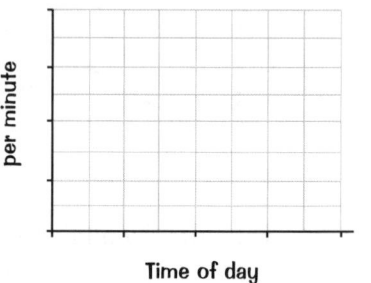

Don't forget about the scales on your graph.

Q5 The table shows the average daytime summer **temperatures** in different habitats around the world.

Habitat	Temperature (°C)
Forest	19
Arctic	0
Desert	32
Grassland	22
Rainforest	27

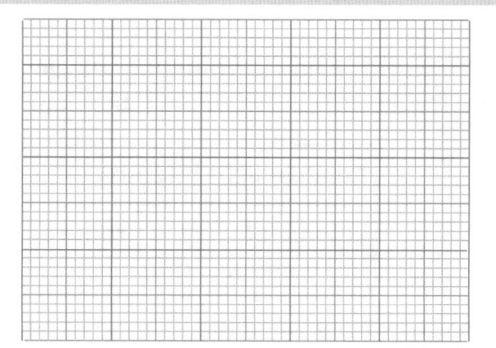

a) Plot a **bar chart** for these results on the grid.

b) From the values for temperature, in which area would you expect fewest plants to grow?

....

c) Suggest a reason for your answer above using the terms **enzymes** and **photosynthesis**.

....

....

Q6 Farmer Fred doesn't put his cows out during the winter because the grass is **not growing**.

a) Give **two** differences between summer and winter conditions that affect the rate of photosynthesis.

....

b) How are the rate of photosynthesis and the growth rate of the grass related?

....

....

Module B7 — Further Biology

Plants and Respiration

Q1 Part of the **word equation** for one type of **respiration** is shown below.

Complete the equation for respiration.

.... + glucose → .... + ... + ...

Q2 The graph below shows the **oxygen** and **carbon dioxide** levels near a plant. The concentration of each gas was measured next to the leaves as the **light intensity** increased.

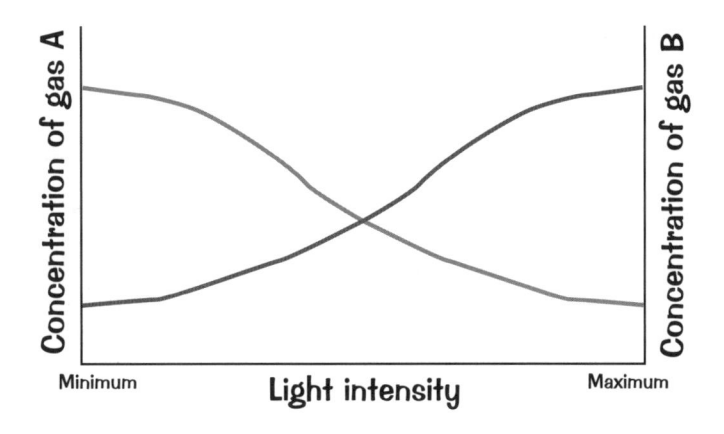

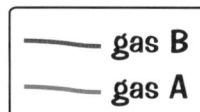

a) i) Which gas is oxygen and which is carbon dioxide?

Gas A is ....

Gas B is ....

ii) Explain how you decided.

....

....

b) State the relationships between the following:

i) the light intensity and the concentration of carbon dioxide.

....

....

ii) the light intensity and the concentration of oxygen.

....

....

Module B7 — Further Biology

Plants and Respiration

Q3 The graph below shows the **carbon dioxide** exchanged by a plant in a 24-hour period.

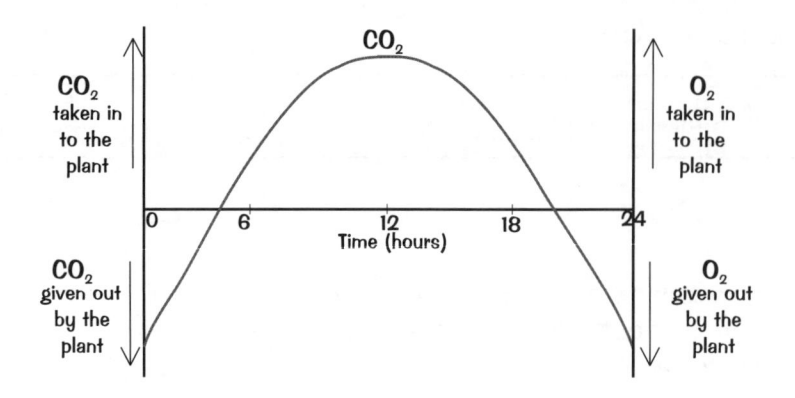

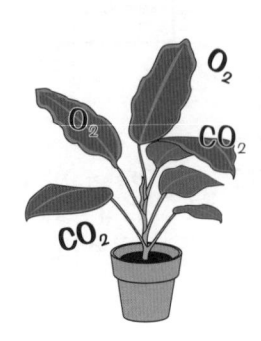

a) **i)** Explain the term **compensation point**.

....

ii) How many times is the compensation point reached in a 24-hour period?

....

iii) Use the graph to find an approximate time at which a compensation point is reached.

....

b) At what time was the rate of photosynthesis highest?

....

c) Sketch a line on the graph to show how the amount of oxygen exchanged by the plant would vary.

Q4 A diagram of a **specialised plant cell** is shown.

a) Name the type of cell shown. ....

b) What is the main **function** of this type of cell?

....

c) Explain why minerals are **not** usually absorbed from the soil by the process of **diffusion**.

....

....

d) Explain how these specialised cells absorb minerals from the soil.
Use the words **active transport**, **concentration**, **respiration** and **energy** in your answer.

....

....

Module B7 — Further Biology

Humans and the Atmosphere

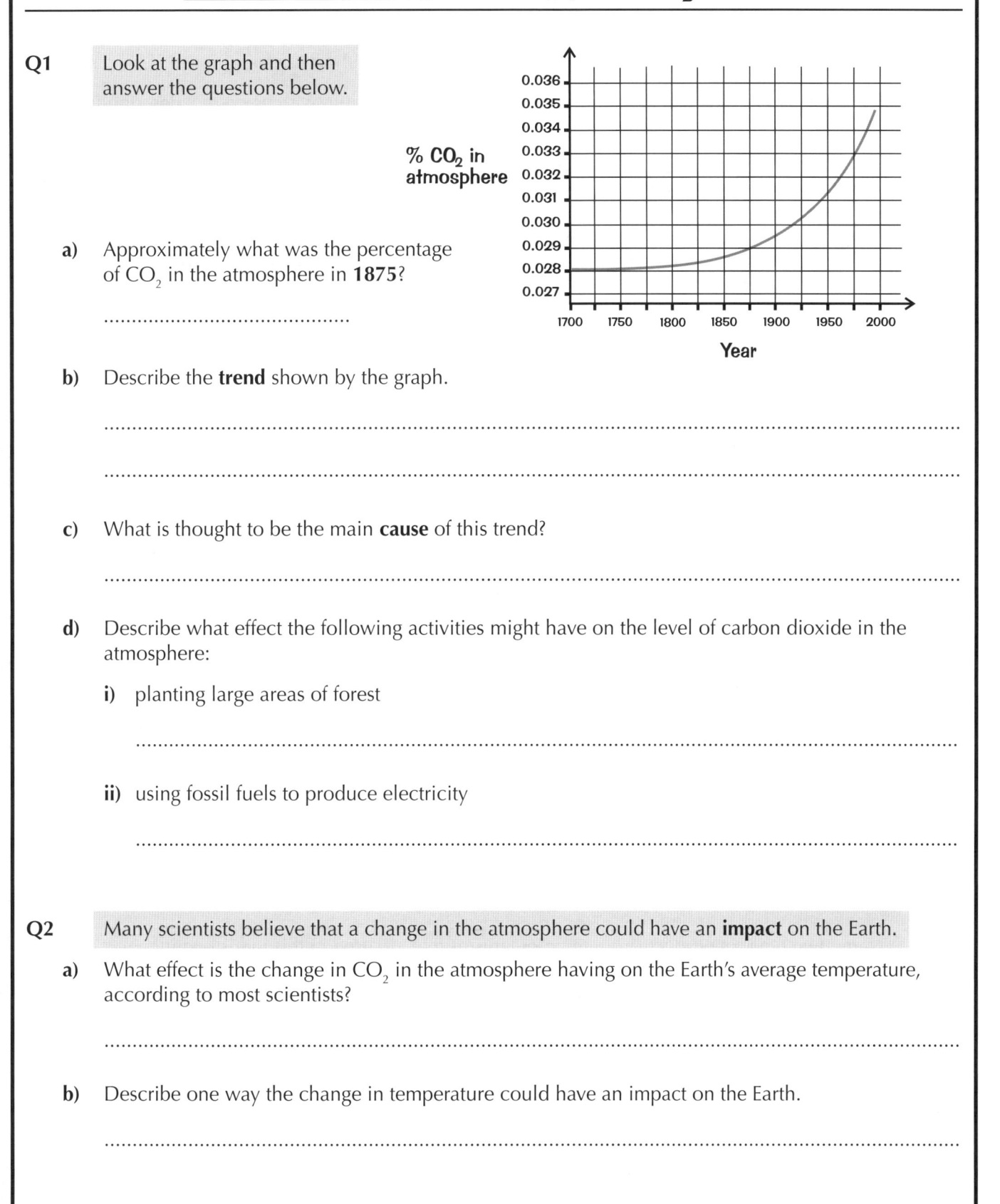

Q1 Look at the graph and then answer the questions below.

a) Approximately what was the percentage of CO_2 in the atmosphere in **1875**?

....

b) Describe the **trend** shown by the graph.

....

....

c) What is thought to be the main **cause** of this trend?

....

d) Describe what effect the following activities might have on the level of carbon dioxide in the atmosphere:

i) planting large areas of forest

....

ii) using fossil fuels to produce electricity

....

Q2 Many scientists believe that a change in the atmosphere could have an **impact** on the Earth.

a) What effect is the change in CO_2 in the atmosphere having on the Earth's average temperature, according to most scientists?

....

b) Describe one way the change in temperature could have an impact on the Earth.

....

Top Tips: Levels of carbon dioxide in the atmosphere are measured by scientists all around the world, to give us an accurate picture of what's happening. One of the main testing sites is on Mauna Loa in Hawaii. Sounds like a great excuse for scientists to have sneaky holidays in the sun to me.

Module B7 — Further Biology

Biotechnology

Q1 Bacteria can be grown on a large scale to help us make **useful products**.

Draw lines to match each label from this diagram of a bacterium with its correct description.

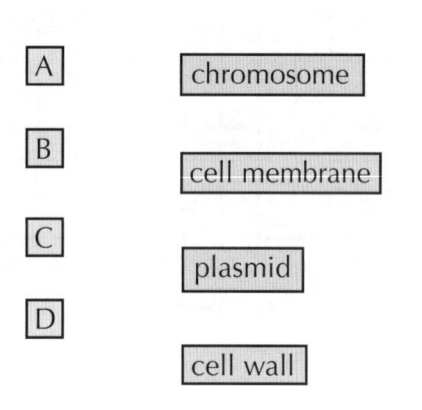

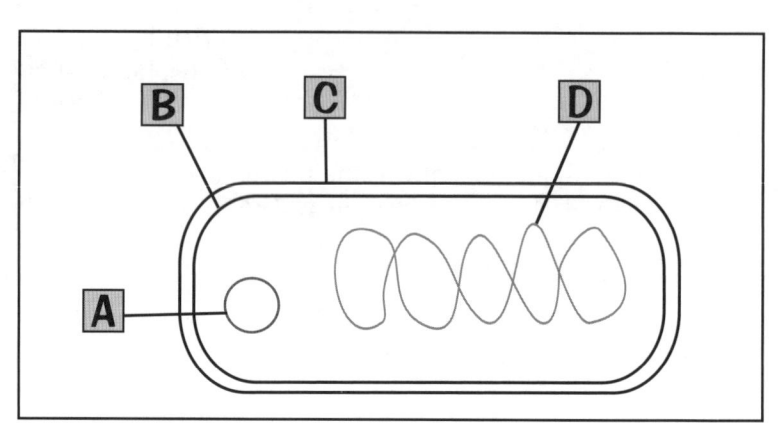

A   chromosome
B   cell membrane
C   plasmid
D   cell wall

Q2 Charlotte works for a company that uses microorganisms to produce **drugs**. She grows bacteria on a large scale and collects their products.

a) Suggest one type of drug that Charlotte's company could manufacture using microorganisms.

....

b) How are microorganisms grown on a **large scale**?

....

c) Name another type of microorganism (not bacteria) that humans can obtain useful products from.

....

Q3 Microorganisms are widely used in the **food industry**.

Name **two** types of products from microorganisms that are used in this industry and briefly explain what each is used for.

1. ....

   ....

2. ....

   ....

> **Top Tips:** We can produce huge amounts of microorganisms and their products. Microorganisms need nutrients and some need oxygen to grow — these are simply added into the mix. They're kept at just the right temperature too, helping to maximise production. Happy little microbes...

Module B7 — Further Biology

Genetic Modification

Q1 **Genetic modification** can be used to change organisms to make them more useful.

a) Put these stages of genetic modification in order by numbering them 1–4.

☐ The vector inserts the gene into the host DNA of the organism.

☐ The desired gene is identified.

☐ The gene is inserted into a vector using ligase.

☐ The desired gene is cut from DNA using restriction enzymes.

Pimp my genes — the ultimate in genetic modification.

b) Name **two** types of vectors.

1. ....

2. ....

Q2 **Plants** can be genetically modified.

a) Describe how genetic modification can improve crop yields.

....

b) Give **two** reasons why some people have concerns about genetically modified plants.

....

....

c) Suggest how genetic modification could help people get the nutrients they need.

....

....

Q3 Bacteria can be genetically modified to make **drugs** and **hormones**.

a) Name a hormone that can be produced by genetically modified bacteria.

....

b) Suggest an **advantage** of using bacteria to produce hormones.

....

Top Tips: Genetically modified crops often get a bad press, but they can be really useful too. It's difficult to know whether to eat them or not — the best thing to do is learn as much as you can about them so you can base your decision on facts, not on scare stories.

Module B7 — Further Biology

Genetic Modification

Q4 Read the following passage about **genetically modified crops** and then answer the questions that follow.

The GM Crop Debate Continues

Genetic modification has been a controversial issue since genetically modified (GM) crops were first introduced for commercial production in 1996. Despite this, by 2001 GM crops covered more than 109.2 million acres worldwide. U.S. farmers are by far the largest producers of GM or 'biotech' crops, producing over 60% of GM crops worldwide. The main crops include corn, soybeans and cotton. The table below shows the percentage of crops planted in the U.S. in 2001 that were genetically modified.

Crop	% of planted crops that were GM in U.S. in 2001
corn	26
soybean	68
cotton	69

The debate about these genetically modified crops continues to rage despite the fact that they are already grown in huge numbers. Currently, there are no genetically modified crops that have been approved for commercial cultivation in the UK.

The benefits of growing GM crops seem clear to the U.S. farming community, which is thought to save millions of dollars each year by using pest-resistant crops rather than chemical pesticides. Some GM crops that are resistant to certain diseases have been developed. Plant diseases caused by viruses, fungi, bacteria and plant nematodes are involved in significant crop losses each year. A certain type of worm causes an estimated $7 billion in annual crop losses in the U.S. However, damage from insects is thought to be even more severe.

Some 22% of the GM crops produced worldwide are varieties developed to be resistant to insects. This can be done by inserting a synthetic version of a gene that produces a toxin, from the naturally occurring soil bacterium, *Bacillus thuringiensis,* into a plant. The plant then produces the toxin to destroy insects. Insect-resistant Bt maize, cotton and potatoes are already grown extensively.

Scientists are still unsure about the effect of GM crops on wildlife and biodiversity. A study by Iowa State University in the U.S. has reported that pollen from GM corn is toxic to monarch caterpillars in the laboratory. The caterpillars were seven times more likely to die when they ate plants dusted with pollen from GM corn rather than normal corn. However, other studies have produced conflicting data.

The effect on wildlife is only one of the many arguments against the growing of GM crops. There is an increasing worry that the genetic material from GM crops will be transferred into wild plants, creating so-called 'superweeds'. Also, many believe that only the multinational biotech companies will reap the rewards from producing GM crops. However, some GM crops such as Golden rice, which can increase levels of Vitamin A in the body, have been designed for people in countries where malnutrition is rife.

As the advantages and disadvantages of growing genetically modified crops become increasingly clear, the problem is deciding whether this is still a risk we are willing to take.

Module B7 — Further Biology

Genetic Modification

a) What is the main benefit to farmers of using GM crops?

....

b) The majority of some crop types grown in the US are GM varieties.
Give an example of one of these crop types.

....

c) Tick the boxes to show whether each statement is **true** or **false**.   True   False

   i) The UK is the largest producer of GM crops.   ☐ ☐

   ii) In 2001 there were more than 109.2 million acres of GM crops worldwide.   ☐ ☐

   iii) Insect-resistant plants are produced by inserting genes from insects.   ☐ ☐

   iv) The study shows that GM corn will kill monarch butterflies if it's grown in fields.   ☐ ☐

d) Despite public concern, the multinational biotech companies are continuing to develop GM crops. Suggest a reason why.

....

e) Suggest **two** reasons why a farmer might not want to change to using GM crops.

   1. ....

   2. ....

f) What percentage of GM crops are thought to be insect-resistant?

....

g) State **one** way that the development of GM crops has benefited society.

....

h) Explain what is meant by the name **Bt maize**.

....

....

....

i) Suggest **two** reasons why the accidental creation of 'superweeds' is a cause for concern.

   1. ....

   2. ....

Module B7 — Further Biology

DNA Technology — Genetic Testing

Q1 Genetic testing can be used to identify **two types** of genetic disorders.

a) Draw lines to match the type of disorder with the correct description.

- a chromosome abnormality
- a faulty gene

- a gene that has a different sequence of bases to the normal gene
- the wrong number of chromosomes

b) Where is DNA commonly obtained from for genetic testing?

....

Q2 **Gene probes** are often used in genetic testing.

a) i) What is a gene probe?

....

ii) How can gene probes locate a specific gene?

....

b) Number the boxes (1-4) to show how a gene probe is used to identify a faulty gene.

- ☐ The chemical tag is located on the DNA.
- ☐ The gene probe is mixed with DNA.
- ☐ A gene probe is produced with a chemical tag attached.
- ☐ The gene probe sticks to the gene.

Q3 **Chemical tags** can be used to **locate** gene probes.

Name **two** types of chemical tags and describe how each one can be located.

1. ....

2. ....

Top Tips: Technology is moving fast, so the techniques used to test for genetic disorders are continually improving. Genetic testing sounds great, but like with lots of things these days it comes with a whole host of social and ethical issues... which you should've covered in module B1.

Module B7 — Further Biology